The **Essential** Buyer's Guide

MORRIS

MINOR & 1000

Saloons, Travellers & Convertibles
1952 to 1971

Your marque expert: Ray Newell

VELOCE PUBLISHING
THE PUBLISHER OF FINE AUTOMOTIVE BOOKS

Also from Veloce Publishing

SpeedPro Series
4-Cylinder Engine – How to Blueprint & Build a Short Block for High Performance (Hammill)
Alfa Romeo DOHC High-Performance Manual (Kartalamakis)
Alfa Romeo V6 Engine High-Perfomance Manual (Kartalamakis)
BMC 998cc A-Series Engine – How to Power Tune (Hammill)
1275cc A-Series High-Performance Manual (Hammill)
Camshafts – How to Choose & Time them for Maximum Power (Hammill)
Cylinder Heads – How to Build, Modify & Power Tune Updated & Revised Edition (Burgess & Gollan)
Distributor-type Ignition Systems – How to Build & Power Tune (Hammill)
Fast Road Car – How to Plan and Build Revised & Updated Colour New Edition (Stapleton)
Ford SOHC 'Pinto' & Sierra Cosworth DOHC Engines – How to Power Tune Updated & Enlarged Edition (Hammill)
Ford V8 – How to Power Tune Small Block Engines (Hammill)
Harley-Davidson Evolution Engines – How to Build & Power Tune (Hammill)
Holley Carburetors – How to Build & Power Tune Revised & Updated Edition (Hammill)
Jaguar XK Engines – How to Power Tune Revised & Updated Colour Edition (Hammill)
MG Midget & Austin-Healey Sprite – How to Power Tune Updated & Revised Edition (Stapleton)
MGB 4-Cylinder Engine – How to Power Tune (Burgess)
MGB V8 Power – How to Give Your Third, Colour Edition (Williams)
MGB, MGC & MGB V8 – How to Improve (Williams)
Mini Engines – How to Power Tune on a Small Budget Colour Edition (Hammill)
Motorsport – Getting Started (Collins)
Nitrous Oxide High-Performance Manual (Langfield)
Rover V8 Engines – How to Power Tune (Hammill)
Sportscar/Kitcar Suspension & Brakes – How to Build & Modify Enlarged & Updated 2nd Edition (Hammill)
SU Carburettor High-Performance Manual (Hammill)
Suzuki 4x4 – How to Modify for Serious Off-Road Action (Richardson)
Tiger Avon Sportscar – How to Build Your Own Updated & Revised 2nd Edition (Dudley)
TR2, 3 & TR4 – How to Improve (Williams)
TR5, 250 & TR6 – How to Improve (Williams)
TR7 & TR8, How to Improve (Williams)
V8 Engine – How to Build a Short Block for High Performance (Hammill)
Volkswagen Beetle Suspension, Brakes & Chassis – How to Modify for High Performance (Hale)
Volkswagen Bus Suspension, Brakes & Chassis – How to Modify for High Performance (Hale)
Weber DCOE, & Dellorto DHLA Carburetors – How to Build & Power Tune 3rd Edition (Hammill)

Those were the days ... Series
Alpine Trials & Rallies 1910-1973 (Pfundner)
Austerity Motoring (Bobbitt)
Brighton National Speed Trials (Gardiner)
British Police Cars (Walker)
Crystal Palace by (Collins)
Dune Buggy Phenomenon (Hale)
Dune Buggy Phenomenon Volume 2 (Hale)
MG's Abingdon Factory (Moylan)
Motor Racing at Brands Hatch in the Seventies (Parker)
Motor Racing at Goodwood in the Sixties (Gardiner)
Motor Racing at Oulton Park in the 60s (McFadyen)
Three Wheelers

Enthusiast's Restoration Manual Series
Citroën 2CV, How to Restore (Porter)
Classic Car Bodywork, How to Restore (Thaddeus)
Classic Car Electrics (Thaddeus)
Classic Cars, How to Paint (Thaddeus)
Reliant Regal, How to Restore (Payne)
Triumph TR2/3/3A, How to Restore (Williams)
Triumph TR4/4A, How to Restore (Williams)
Triumph TR5/250 & 6, How to Restore (Williams)
Triumph TR7/8, How to Restore (Williams)
Volkswagen Beetle, How to Restore (Tyler)
Yamaha FS1-E, How to Restore (Watts)

Essential Buyer's Guide Series
Alfa GT (Booker)
Alfa Romeo Spider Giulia (Booker)
Citroën 2CV (Paxton)
Jaguar E-type 3.8 & 4.2-litre (Crespin)
Jaguar E-type V12 5.3-litre (Crespin)
MGB & MGB GT (Williams)
Mercedes-Benz 280SL-560SL Roadsters (Bass)
Mercedes-Benz 'Pagoda' 230SL, 250SL & 280SL Roadsters & Coupés (Bass)
Morris Minor (Newell)
Porsche 928 (Hemmings)

Triumph TR6 (Williams)
VW Beetle (Cservenka & Copping)
VW Bus (Cservenka & Copping)

Auto-Graphics Series
Fiat-based Abarths (Sparrow)
Jaguar Mkl & Il Saloons (Sparrow)
Lambretta Ll series scooters (Sparrow)

Rally Giants Series
Big Healey – 100-Six & 3000 (Robson)
Ford Escort Mkl (Robson)
Lancia Stratos (Robson)
Peugeot 205 T16 (Robson)
Subaru Impreza (Robson)

General
1½-litre GP Racing 1961-1965 (Whitelock)
AC Two-litre Saloons & Buckland Sportscars (Archibald)
Alfa Romeo Giulia Coupé GT & GTA (Tipler)
Alfa Tipo 33 (McDonough & Collins)
Anatomy of the Works Minis (Moylan)
Armstrong-Siddeley (Smith)
Autodrome (Collins & Ireland)
Automotive A-Z, Lane's Dictionary of Automotive Terms (Lane)
Automotive Mascots (Kay & Springate)
Bahamas Speed Weeks, The (O'Neil)
Bentley Continental, Corniche and Azure (Bennett)
Bentley MkIV, Rolls-Royce Silver Wraith, Dawn & Cloud/Bentley R & S-series (Nutland)
BMC Competitions Department Secrets (Turner, Chambers & Browning)
BMW 5-Series (Cranswick)
BMW Z-Cars (Taylor)
British 250cc Racing Motorcycles by Chris Pereira
British Cars, The Complete Catalogue of, 1895-1975 (Culshaw & Horrobin)
BRM – a mechanic's tale (Salmon)
BRM V16 (Ludvigsen)
Bugatti Type 40 (Price)
Bugatti 46/50 Updated Edition (Price & Arbey)
Bugatti T44 & T49 (Price & Arbey)
Bugatti 57 2nd Edition (Price)
Caravans, The Illustrated History 1919-1959 (Jenkinson)
Caravans, The Illustrated History from 1960 (Jenkinson)
Chrysler 300 – America's Most Powerful Car 2nd Edition (Ackerson)
Citroën DS (Bobbitt)
Cobra – The Real Thing! (Legate)
Cortina – Ford's Bestseller (Robson)
Coventry Climax Racing Engines (Hammill)
Daimler SP250 'Dart' New Edition (Long)
Datsun Fairlady Roadster to 280ZX – The Z-car Story (Long)
Dino – The V6 Ferrari (Long)
Dodge Dynamite! (Grist)
Drive on the Wild Side – 20 extreme driving adventures from around the world, A (Weaver)
Ducati 750 Bible, The (Falloon)
Dune Buggy, Building a – The Essential Manual (Shakespeare)
Dune Buggy Files (Hale)
Dune Buggy Handbook (Hale)
Edward Turner: the man behind the motorcycles (Clew)
Fiat & Abarth 124 Spider & Coupé (Tipler)
Fiat & Abarth 500 & 600 2nd edition (Bobbitt)
Fiats, Great Small (Ward)
Ford F100/F150 Pick-up 1948-1996 (Ackerson)
Ford F150 1997-2005 (Ackerson)
Ford GT – Then, and Now (Streather)
Ford GT40 (Legate)
Ford in Miniature (Olson)
Ford Model Y (Roberts)
Ford Thunderbird from 1954, The Book of the (Long)
Funky Mopeds (Skelton)
GT – The World's Best GT Cars 1953-73 (Dawson)
Hillclimbing & sprinting (Short)
Honda NSX (Long)
Jaguar, The Rise of (Price)
Jaguar XJ-S (Long)
Jeep CJ (Ackerson)
Jeep Wrangler (Ackerson)
Karmann-Ghia Coupé & Convertible (Bobbitt)
Lambretta Bible, The (Davies)
Lancia Delta HF Integrale (Blaettel & Wagner)
Land Rover, The Half-Ton Military (Cook)
Laverda Twins & Triples Bible 1968-1986 (Falloon)
Lea-Francis Story, The (Price)
Lexus Story, The (Long)
Lola – The Illustrated History (1957-1977) (Starkey)
Lola – All the Sports Racing & Single-Seater Racing Cars 1978-1997 (Starkey)
Lola T70 – The Racing History & Individual Chassis Record 3rd Edition (Starkey)
Lotus 49 (Oliver)

Marketing Mobiles, The Wonderful Wacky World of (Hale)
Mazda MX-5/Miata 1.6 Enthusiast's Workshop Manual (Grainger & Shoemark)
Mazda MX-5/Miata 1.8 Enthusiast's Workshop Manual (Grainger & Shoemark)
Mazda MX-5 Miata: the book of the world's favourite sportscar (Long)
Mazda MX-5 Miata Roadster (Long)
MGA (Price Williams)
MGB & MGB GT – Expert Guide (Auto-Doc Series) (Williams)
MGB Electrical Systems (Astley)
Micro Caravans (Jenkinson)
Microcars at large! (Quellin)
Mini Cooper – The Real Thing! (Tipler)
Mitsubishi Lancer Evo, the road car & WRC story (Long)
Monthléry, the story of the Paris autodrome (Boddy)
Moto Guzzi Sport & Le Mans Bible (Falloon)
Motor Movies – The Posters! (Veysey)
Motor Racing – Reflections of a Lost Era (Carter)
Motorcycle Road & Racing Chassis Designs (Knoakes)
Motorhomes, The Illustrated History (Jenkinson)
Motorsport in colour, 1950s (Wainwright)
Nissan 300ZX & 350Z – The Z-Car Story (Long)
Pass the Theory and Practical Driving Tests (Gibson & Hoole)
Pontiac Firebird (Cranswick)
Porsche Boxster (Long)
Porsche 356 (Long)
Porsche 911 Carrera – The Last of the Evolution (Corlett)
Porsche 911R, RS & RSR, 4th Edition (Starkey)
Porsche 911 – The Definitive History 1963-1971 (Long)
Porsche 911 – The Definitive History 1971-1977 (Long)
Porsche 911 – The Definitive History 1977-1987 (Long)
Porsche 911 – The Definitive History 1987-1997 (Long)
Porsche 911 – The Definitive History 1997-2004 (Long)
Porsche 911SC 'Super Carrera' – The Essential Companion (Streather)
Porsche 914 & 914-6: The Definitive History Of The Road & Competition Cars (Long)
Porsche 924 (Long)
Porsche 944 (Long)
Porsche 993 'King of Porsche' – The Essential Companion (Streather)
Porsche Racing Cars – 1953 to 1975 (Long)
Porsche Racing Cars – 1976 on (Long)
Porsche – The Rally Story (Meredith)
Porsche: Three Generations of Genius (Meredith)
RAC Rally Action! (Gardiner)
Rallye Sport Fords: the inside story (Moreton)
Redman, Jim – 6 Times World Motorcycle Champion: The Autobiography (Redman)
Rolls-Royce Silver Shadow/Bentley T Series Corniche & Camargue Revised & Enlarged Edition (Bobbitt)
Rolls-Royce Silver Spirit, Silver Spur & Bentley Mulsanne 2nd Edition (Bobbitt)
RX-7 – Mazda's Rotary Engine Sportscar (updated & revised new edition) (Long)
Scooters & Microcars, The A-Z of popular (Dan)
Singer Story: Cars, Commercial Vehicles, Bicycles & Motorcycles (Atkinson)
SM – Citroën's Maserati-engined Supercar (Long & Claverol)
Subaru Impreza: the road car and WRC story (Long)
Taxi! The Story of the 'London' Taxicab (Bobbitt)
Toyota Celica & Supra (Long)
Toyota MR2 Coupés & Spyders (Long)
Triumph Motorcycles & the Meriden Factory (Hancox)
Triumph Speed Twin & Thunderbird Bible (Woolridge)
Triumph Tiger Cub Bible (Estall)
Triumph Trophy Bible (Woolridge)
Triumph TR6 (Kimberley)
Unraced (Collins)
Velocette Motorcycles – MSS to Thruxton Updated & Revised (Burris)
Virgil Exner – Visioneer: The official biography of Virgil M Exner designer extraordinaire (Grist)
Volkswagen Bus Book, The (Bobbitt)
Volkswagen Bus or Van to Camper, How to Convert (Porter)
Volkswagens of the World (Glen)
VW Beetle Cabriolet (Bobbitt)
VW Beetle – The Car of the 20th Century (Copping)
VW Bus – 40 years of Splitties, Bays & Wedges (Copping)
VW Bus Book, The (Bobbitt)
VW Golf: five generations of fun (Copping & Cservenka)
VW – The air-cooled era (Copping)
VW T5 Camper Conversion Manual (Porter)
VW Campers (Copping)
Works Minis, The Last (Purves & Brenchley)
Works Rally Mechanic (Moylan)

www.veloce.co.uk

First published in April 2007 by Veloce Publishing Limited, 33 Trinity Street, Dorchester DT1 1TT, England. Fax 01305 268864/e-mail info@veloce.co.uk/ web www.veloce.co.uk or www.velocebooks.com
ISBN 978-1-845841-01-0. UPC: 6-36847-04101-4.
Readers with ideas for automotive books, or books on other transport or related hobby subjects, are invited to write to the editorial director of Veloce Publishing at the above address.
British Library Cataloguing in Publication Data – A catalogue record for this book is available from the British Library. Typesetting, design and page make-up all by Veloce Publishing Ltd on Apple Mac.
Printed in India by Replika Press.

Introduction & thanks
– the purpose of this book

The purpose of this book is to provide an insight into the joys and pitfalls associated with buying a Morris Minor. Whilst never losing sight of the enduring charm and character that the Morris Minor has, the rose tinted spectacles will be dispensed with, and every facet of buying, owning and driving one of these classic vehicles will be scrutinised. Guidance, based on the author's thirty-plus years of practical experience of owning and driving all of the models, will allow you to determine which vehicle is the right one for you; more importantly, this book will provide you with a guide to assessing the condition and practicalities associated with purchasing, owning and maintaining the vehicle you buy. From determining basic considerations such as whether the car of your choice will fit in your garage, to providing an in-depth guide of what to look for when assessing a specific vehicle, it's all here. A straightforward points system allows you to objectively evaluate the relative merits of any potential purchase.

Classic lines of the Morris 1000.

Running costs are considered too, with the inclusion of an invaluable guide to parts availability for various models, along with an at-a-glance chart detailing what you might expect to pay for routine servicing and key components.

Redoubtable A-Series engine.

Tens of thousands of vehicles survive worldwide and while this provides for a wide range of choice, it means that if you have a particular interest in one type of vehicle, then you can be reassured that someone, somewhere will share that interest. This helpful guide, along with the experience of former and present owners, will enable prospective buyers to get the best vehicle for their money, regardless of budget. In doing so, it will help achieve the universal aim of owners throughout the world, which is to ensure the continued use and preservation of the post-war Morris Minor.

Central speedometer; a feature since 1954.

Whether it be a challenging basket case for restoration, a daily driver, or a top-notch concours car, this Buyer's Guide will be an invaluable resource.

Thanks

Thanks are due to a number of people who assisted in various ways in the production of this book: Liz Saxon, Yvonne Harrison, Andrew Stone, Martin O'Dowd and David Brown.

Photographs: I am indebted to John Colley for his assistance and permission to reproduce the majority of the photographs. Thanks also go to Ted and Clare Connolly, Sandy Hamilton, and Robert O'Dowd for additional photography.

Contents

Publisher's note
Throughout this book the model name Morris Minor can be taken to include the Morris 1000, except where the models are being described separately.

Essential Buyer's Guide™ currency
At the time of publication a BG unit of currency "●" equals approximately £1.00/US$2.00/Euro 1.50. Please adjust to suit current exchange rates.

1 Is it the right car for you?
– marriage guidance

Tall and short drivers
Seat adjustment fore and aft allows for all but the tallest drivers to be accommodated. Those short of stature may need to have the driver's seat in Morris 1000 models raised at the rear to allow for safe access to the pedal controls and improve forward visibility. Larger framed individuals may find the relatively small distance between the steering wheel and the seat squab challenging.

Weight of controls
Power steering passed the Minor by. However, the highly rated rack and pinion system allowed for positive and direct steering. Drum brakes all round are adequate but additional pedal pressure is needed compared to modern cars.

Will it fit in the garage?
All versions of the Morris Minor will easily fit into the smallest of garages. At 12ft 5in (3m 76cm) long, 5ft 0in (1m 52cm) high, and 5ft 0in (1m 55cm) wide, the compact dimensions are a real asset.

Interior space
Saloon, Convertible and Traveller models all comfortably accommodate four adults. Headroom is good and access to the rear seats is facilitated on two-door, Convertible and Traveller models by folding or forward tipping front seats.

Luggage capacity
On Saloon and Convertible models, luggage capacity is compromised slightly by the sloping contours of the boot (trunk) lid. However, this is compensated for by the facility to fold down the rear seat. Traveller models have a similar arrangement, which provides for an even greater capacity when one or two passengers are present.

Running costs
Morris Minors are economical to run with good fuel economy. Average fuel consumption ranges from 35 to 43mpg.

Usability
Morris 1000 models are more than capable of being used as daily transport. Earlier Series II 803cc models in standard specification are more pedestrian in terms of performance. Original lighting and semaphore indicators can present problems and many owners have changed this, in an effort to increase safety. Standard front seats from 1956 onwards are not the most comfortable for extended journeys.

Parts availability

The Morris 1000 models are very well provided for. Virtually all parts are readily obtainable and there is an excellent network of suppliers. Earlier models, pre-1956, are not so well catered for, though clubs like the Morris Minor Owners Club seek to source rare parts, and even commissions the re-manufacture of some.

Parts costs

There is a competitive market for Morris 1000 parts. Shop around for the best bargains and prices. Earlier parts exclusive to Series II models (1952-1956) command higher prices.

Insurance group

Low group insurance for standard models. Enthusiasts would recommend an agreed value classic/collector's policy for best value, and added protection in the event of a claim. A variety of mileage options are available and various companies offer this. The Morris Minor Owners Club has a recommended scheme.

Investment potential

Morris Minor prices across the board have been stable for some time. New buyers are unlikely to lose out if they acquire sound, well-maintained vehicles. It should be noted that restoration costs can far outweigh any subsequent retail sale value. Concours vehicles are in a price league of their own. Auction prices and commercial values may not reflect the intrinsic value to the owner.

Foibles

Rear end axle tramp (hopping) when cornering at speed (1098cc models). Distinctive sound of exhaust on overrun is a quirky feature.

Plus points

Distinctive British classic vehicle, easy to maintain, economical to run and full of character.

Minus points

Ventilation is quite poor on early models, and they have a tendency to steam up when it is wet. Pre-1956 models have ineffective wipers. Some of the vulnerable areas for rust are not immediately visible – panels need to be removed to see the full extent of possible problems. Some Convertible models are post-production 2-door Saloon conversions!

Alternatives

For any Morris Minor enthusiast there is probably no real viable alternative. From a British perspective, alternatives might include the Austin A30/A35 or the Austin A40. The obvious overseas alternative is the equally iconic Volkswagen Beetle.

2 Cost considerations
– affordable, or a money pit?

Recommended service intervals reflect contemporary custom and practice when vehicles were in production. 3000 and 6000 mile service intervals are advisable.

Small service: ● x50
Engine service kit: ● x14
Large service: ● x75
New clutch (not fitted): 803/948cc ● x100; 1098cc ● x90; (fitted) ● x175
Full engine (not fitted): ● x650
Rebuilt gearbox: 803cc ● x265; 948cc ● x235; 1098cc ● x215
Unleaded cylinder head conversion (not fitted): ● x185; (fitted) ● x295
Brake drum: ● x20
Brake shoes: ● x12
Brake master cylinder (not fitted): ● x50
Brake wheel cylinders: front 803cc ● x60; 948c/1098cc ● x10; rear 803cc ● x25; 948cc/1098cc ● x12
Sealed beam headlight unit: ● x25
Rear lamp base (no lens): 803cc ● x25; 948cc ● x30; 1098cc ● x38
Rear lamp lens: early 803cc ● x20; late 803cc ● x15; 948cc ● x10; 1098cc ● x15
Exhaust system (not fitted): mild steel ● x27; stainless steel ● x60

Steering rack (reconditioned): ● x33
Bumper blades: ● x70
Carburettor (new): ● x95
Fuel pump (SU) (new): ● x75
Front wing (fender): Heritage approved ● x120; reproduction ● x60
Rear wing (fender): Heritage approved saloon ● x100; reproduction ● x60
Heritage approved rear wing (fender): Traveller ● x90
Fuel tank: Heritage produced ● x200
Windscreen seal: ● x19
Wiring loom, braided: ● x95
Seat straps (12 per seat): ● x1.25 each
Full respray (including preparation): ● x1500
Traveller wood kit complete: ● x1200; fitting ● x800
Main centre crossmember: ● x50
Basket case restoration (professional): ● x5-6k; ● x10k plus for concours standard
Convertible hoods: vinyl ● x150; mohair ● x450

Parts that are easy to find: Body parts for later models, repair panels, interior trim, service items and most mechanical parts.

Parts that are difficult to find: Model specific body panels for pre-1956 vehicles, some gearbox components, early steering wheels, chrome windscreen inserts for pre-1956 models.

Parts that are very expensive: New old stock items for early cars, complete Traveller wood kit, early light units. Original specification crossply tyres.

Most chrome parts are still available too!

Repair and replacement body parts are widely available.

7

3 Living with a Morris Minor
– will you get along together?

Owning a Morris Minor is akin to having an additional family member. This fact is borne out by the reluctance encountered when former long-standing owners come to the point of parting with their pride and joy ... regardless of its condition. Pet names are not uncommon, such is the affinity between owner and said Morris Minor. The tradition is catching, so be warned if you are a prospective first time buyer. Once described as the 'poor man's Rolls Royce', the Minor is an unpretentious vehicle. Its owners reflect all sections of society, regardless of age or background.

An important consideration in any purchase will be the anticipated amount of use and whether the vehicle is to be used as daily transport. If the vehicle is being used in standard specification, the later 1098cc models are more suited to the demands of traffic in the 21st century. Improved performance, larger brakes, better lighting, marginally better heating and ventilation, and a few safety features, including toughened glass, all combine to make the vehicles built between 1962 and 1971 a safer bet. Mechanically, there is little to choose between the 948cc and 1098cc powered models save for a slight increase in acceleration and top end speed. All Morris Minors are bereft of synchromesh on first gear so driving style has to be modified accordingly. For the more adventurous driver this may include mastering the art of 'double-declutching'.

One should not totally discount the pre-1956 models as daily drivers. Few owners consistently use these vehicles as everyday transport unless the vehicle has been seriously uprated in terms of mechanical specification and lighting, including supplementary methods of indication. With suitable modifications, a sound Series II can provide reliable transport, particularly in spring and summer when the warmer temperatures circumvent difficulties with heating and ventilation. Extended motorway use is probably best avoided in these vehicles.

The spacious interior of the Traveller.

One of the virtues of the Morris Minor range is the fact that there is something for everyone. Whether it be the prospect of open air motoring with the Convertible, practical work with a commercial, or simply pottering in a Traveller, the versatility of the Morris Minor comes to the fore. Whatever your lifestyle, there is a Minor to suit. What's more, running costs are very reasonable. Economical motoring has been a trademark feature of these vehicles since their inception. Compared to modern

Simple design – no frills.

vehicles, the Morris Minor still returns a respectable 40mpg when driven sensibly. All vehicles qualify for road fund tax exemption in the UK, given that they are designated as historic vehicles. Cheap insurance with a variety of mileage options linked to agreed value classic vehicle schemes means that essential overheads can be kept at affordable levels. The reassurance that spare parts are

Top down motoring – open air options.

readily available and that there is an active network of traders, enthusiasts and like-minded owners ready to help in the event of any problems, is a real bonus.

For those owners who prefer to do their own servicing and routine maintenance, the Morris Minor is a joy to work on. Unlike most modern day cars, there is room to work in the engine bay. Simplicity was the watchword in the original design and those with a modicum of engineering nous can tackle most mechanical repairs with a fair degree of confidence. The A-Series engine is a robust unit with an excellent reputation for reliability and longevity. It is also easy to work on, and replacement components are readily available. Traveller owners will soon become aware of the need for thorough maintenance of the ash frame which is a structural part of the vehicle. Regular stripping and revarnishing of the wood with a recommended preservative and clear varnish will pay dividends in the long run.

Comfort was not necessarily foremost in Alec Issigonis' mind when he designed the Morris Minor … or the Mini come to that. A legacy of that concept is that even the most modern of Minors had seats which left something to be desired in terms of lumbar support and padding. Consequently, many Morris Minors have had improved seating fitted retrospectively. Fully contoured, adjustable reclining seats from vehicles such as the MG Metro are commonplace in many later Minors which are in more regular use. Other mechanical upgrades are often fitted too. It is not unusual to find disc brake conversions from the Morris Marina, 5-speed gearboxes from Toyota, 1275 MG Midget engines, brake servos and alternator conversions. All of these

are worthwhile additions to improve the comfort and driveability of the Minor, and make it more suitable for everyday use. Many other after-market accessories including more powerful heaters, and heated rear screens are available too. In most cases these items do not detract from the essential character of the original vehicles.

Morris Minor Saloons continued in production until 1970.

Series II Convertible with characteristic split screen and 'cheesegrater' grille.

See Chapter 12 for value assessment. This chapter shows in percentage terms the relative value of individual models in good condition in the UK. Concours cars (in as-new condition or better)

Contrasting painted grille on early Series II Traveller.

will command double or even treble prices, while restoration projects will be worth as little as a tenth. Values for vehicles in other countries will vary enormously.

There are two main considerations to bear in mind when reviewing the model range covering the period 1952-1971. First, the actual model type, two- or four-door Saloon, Convertible or Traveller. Second, the production Series to which the vehicle belongs: Series II 803cc (early or late), Morris Minor 948cc (designated Series III), or Morris 1000 1098cc (designated Series 5).

The combination of these two facets allows for a considerable range of models to choose from. For ease of reference, all body styles will be considered in the sequence they entered production.

Series II. Split windscreen (early type) 1952-1954
Saloons: 803cc. Introduced in August 1952 as four-door Saloon; two-door and Convertible models followed in January 1953. These vehicles were produced alongside the Series MM sidevalve models until February 1953 when the Series MM models were phased out. Initially the change was barely discernible as the same monocoque bodyshell was used. A reshaped bulkhead crossmember was incorporated to accommodate the taller OHV engine. Apart from a change to the bonnet badging, the main changes centred on the adoption of Austin mechanicals – 803cc engine and transmission.

Key features
Split windscreen, 'cheesegrater' grille with vertical slats, trademark gold coloured dash with cluster of gauges directly in front of driver, rexine covered board headlining. Convertible models: fixed rear side windows and hood with small celluloid rear window.
Saloons – **60%**
Convertibles – **85%**

Series II four-door Saloon with revised grille.

Series II Travellers. Split windscreen (early type) 1953-1954

Introduced in October 1953. Designated the Travellers Car in early brochures. Sometimes referred to as a 'Shooting brake'.

Series II Traveller model, ash-framed.

Key features
Unitary construction steel cab and rear floor. Ash-framed rear body incorporating aluminium side, door and roof panels with opening side windows. Folding rear and passenger seats. Traveller models were available in Standard or Deluxe. Deluxe specification included over-ridders, leather interior, passenger side sun visor and a heater. This facility became available to the rest of the range soon after.

Traveller – **100%**

Series II Convertible. Much sought after in original condition.

Series II. Split windscreen. All models (late) 1954-1956

In October 1954, the entire Morris Minor range was subject to a major update.

Key features
Revised front-end arrangement with alterations, grille incorporating horizontal bars and revised lighting. New dash and instrumentation panel with centrally positioned speedometer. Revised seating for Saloon and Convertible models with fixed back instead of folding front seats.

Saloons – **50%**
Convertibles – **85%**
Travellers – **100%**

Morris Minor 1000 two-door. 948cc. Full-sized one-piece screen improved all-round visibility. Morris 1000 was a best seller.

Morris Minor 1000 1956-1962 (948cc)

All models underwent a major transformation in 1956 with the introduction of the Morris 1000 range.

Key features
Revised body styling with single piece windscreen, larger rear screen, narrower windscreen pillars. New style rear wings fitted, uprated mechanical specification with 948cc engine, improved gearbox with remote control and much improved gear ratios. Dished steering wheel. Horn and indicator controls moved to steering column. Fuel tank capacity increased in 1957. Semaphore indicators retained until 1961. Variety of interiors fitted during the period 1956-1962. Convertible models had

Morris 1000 948cc Saloon. Still going strong after all these years.

Rare colours like this Highway Yellow four-door are much sought-after.

Family motoring aided by four-door design.

1966 Morris 1000 Convertible.

hoods fitted with larger rear windows from 1957.
Saloons – **60%**
Convertibles – **80%**
Travellers – **90%**

Morris Minor 1000. 1962-1971 (1098cc)

All models underwent another major revamp in 1962. Body styling remained largely unchanged on all models. The significant change was the introduction of the 1098cc engine. Accompanying changes included a revised gearbox, a larger diameter clutch, improved braking and a change to the axle ratio.

Key features

Early transitional models retain many interior styling features of the 948cc models. This extended to lighting, indication and instrumentation. From 1963, improved lighting with combined rear brake/indicator units and front side/indicator lamps were distinctive features. Wipers work in parallel as opposed to a clap hands action. From 1964, Saloon, Convertible and Traveller models had revised interior trim and fascia and were fitted with seat belts. Late changes (1971) on some Traveller models include steering column locks. Some also had an alternator fitted. Wide choice of paint colours and trim combinations offered.
Saloons – **60%**
Convertibles – **85%**
Travellers – **100%**

Morris 1000 models denoted by Minor 1000 badges.

Traveller model. Highly valued in good condition. Different specifications were used for Travellers supplied to the Armed Forces.

5 Before you view
– be well informed

Do your homework
Research the specifications of the particular model you are looking to buy before you view. If originality is high on your list of priorities, make sure you know what you are looking for. It may seem 'anorakish', but making a checklist of key features may pay dividends in the long run.

Where is the car?
The decision whether to travel substantial distances (200+ miles) to view a Morris Minor will be influenced by the rarity of the vehicle. While it may be worth making the effort to view a rare Series II Convertible or Traveller, the abundance of later Morris Minor 1000 1098cc models could preclude making such a journey, as equally good examples may be available closer to home.

Dealer or private sale?
There are a number of specialist companies which offer Morris Minors for sale. Other general classic car dealers occasionally feature Morris Minors on their stock lists The majority of vehicles offered for sale appear in the classic car press and in club publications as private sales. There is no shortage of vehicles for sale, save for the rarest models. It is always recommended to view private sale vehicles at the home of the vendor rather than at some inhospitable, unknown venue.

Cost of collection and delivery
One of the items often overlooked when acquiring a classic car is the cost associated with collection and delivery. If the vehicle is not roadworthy, or is incapable of being driven legally, it may be necessary to engage the services of a transportation company or hire a car transporter trailer. Such services can be costly. If driving your new purchase is an option then ensuring that adequate insurance cover is in place is a vital consideration. Resist the temptation to drive on temporary third party insurance cover. Instead, secure adequate agreed value insurance.

View – when and where?
Ideally, you should never view a vehicle in the rain or when the light is fading. Return when conditions are better if you are serious about buying. If access to a ramp is available at a local garage and the vendor agrees, be sure to take the opportunity to view the underside.

Reason for sale?
With a specialist garage or dealer, the reason is obvious. However it is always advisable to ask why the vehicle is being sold. If it is a private sale, the answer can be quite illuminating and can occasionally provide a bargaining point in your favour – unfinished project, surplus to requirements, loss of storage, bereavement, etc.

LHD to RHD conversion

With so many RHD vehicles to choose from in the UK, this is not a likely option. It is feasible but not cost-effective ... yet!

Condition

Determining the condition of the vehicle before viewing is more feasible with the continuing advances in digital media. Photographs of the exterior, interior and engine bay may provide sufficient evidence to determine whether further investigation is warranted. The critical area with all Morris Minors is the underside, so close questioning about the amount of repair work done previously may also encourage or deter.

All original specification

Original specification vehicles tend to command higher prices, particularly with owners who view the purchase as a 'collector's car' rather than a daily driver. Some owners may have authentic documentation relating to the factory production record for the vehicle, in the form of a Heritage Certificate. Ask if this will be available to view when you go and see the vehicle.

Matching numbers

The emphasis here should be on the chassis number. On early vehicles, the chassis number is stamped into the bulkhead just below the wiring loom aperture. On later cars it was stamped into the floor on the driver's side front footwell. Finding the numbers on these cars is difficult, particularly if the floor has rusted or repairs have been carried out. A separate chassis plate fitted to the bulkhead should have all the information, including prefix letters and numbers, on it. Engine numbers are stamped on a plate attached to the engine block. Chassis numbers should always be checked to see if they match. With engine numbers this is less critical as many vehicles will have had an engine change. After all, the oldest vehicles date from 1952!

Is the seller the legal owner?

Confirm that the person selling the vehicle is both the legal owner and the registered keeper. If this is not evident, get the legal owner's details and check that he/she is aware that the vehicle is being offered for sale.

Taxed?

All Morris Minors in the UK are tax exempt and have the designation 'Historic Vehicle'. If the vehicle has been off the road for some time, check the status of the SORN declaration (Statutory Off Road Notification). In other countries, is the vehicle currently taxed/licensed for use on the public highway?

Roadworthy?

In the UK, MoT certificates can provide a useful check on the usage of the vehicle over a period of time. Many owners will have previous certificates to authenticate the mileage covered. Remember that a current certificate is only an indication of the condition of the vehicle when it was last tested.

Unleaded conversion
Many Morris Minors have had 'unleaded' cylinder heads fitted (ie: with hardened valve seats for the use of unleaded fuel). For those that haven't, the option is there for the new owner to convert. Alternatively, there is the option of using approved additives. Some vehicles are used quite happily without either, probably to the long-term detriment of the engine if annual mileage is high. It is best to ask some searching questions if presented with this scenario.

How can you pay?
A cheque/check may take several days to clear and the vendor may prefer to have cash. However, a banker's draft (a cheque/check issued by a bank), is as good as cash and far more secure. For UK buyers, a building society cheque is another safe option, but it may take longer to clear.

Buying at auction
If you're considering buying at auction, refer to Chapter 10 for further advice and guidance.

Professional vehicle checks
There are professional companies which will undertake vehicle assessment checks for a fee (hourly rate plus travel costs). Owner's clubs can usually help by putting you in touch with such specialists. Other organisations who undertake evaluations and produce a vehicle report in the UK are –

AA   0800 085 3007 (motoring organisation with vehicle inspectors)
ABS   0800 358 5855 (specialist vehicle inspectors)
RAC   0870 533 3660 (motoring organisation with vehicle inspectors)

Other countries have similar organisations.

6 Inspection equipment
– these items will really help

This book
Using this book as an aide memoire will serve several purposes. It will hopefully ensure that you do not overlook any of the really important parts of the vehicle, and it will also show the vendor that you are taking your purchase seriously and are genuine in your quest for a suitable vehicle.

Magnet
Take a plastic-type fridge magnet with you. They are ideal as they are not too strong and they don't scratch the paintwork. Your aim is to determine whether beneath the shiny paintwork there are areas of filler … which might mean expensive remedial work in the future.

Torch
There are numerous nooks and crannies to investigate thoroughly on all models of the Morris Minor. A torch will be a valuable resource in illuminating the darkest recesses. It will also prove useful when exploring the underside of the vehicle.

Probe (small screwdriver)
A small screwdriver can be used discretely as a probe to investigate corrosion in areas such as the wheelarches, the underside and in the boot. However, extreme caution must be used as it is all too easy to go through areas of weak metal and incur the anger of the vendor in the process.

Overalls
Show you mean business. Be prepared to get dirty as you investigate the underside of the vehicle or check out the mechanical components. Take some disposable rubber/latex gloves along, too.

Reading glasses (if you need them for close work)
Essential if you need to undertake close-up inspections or examine the documentation relating to the vehicle.

Mirror on a stick
An invaluable aid for viewing the underside and sill areas. When fixed at an angle, can provide a useful perspective on some inaccessible areas which otherwise might be missed.

Digital camera
Photograph as many aspects of the vehicle as possible, particularly those that give cause for concern. Later, armed with photographic evidence, you can seek the opinions of others before committing to a purchase.

When looking at a Morris Minor with a serious intent to buy, it is important to be objective and not to be swayed by sentiment or the owner's persuasive sales patter. In the words of an old adage, 'let your head rule your heart'. The fact of the matter is that the Minor's monocoque construction, though durable, is prone to rusting out.

Exterior

When viewing the exterior of the vehicle, remember that paint and bodywork are the most expensive of any repairs you might have to undertake. First impressions are important. Walk towards the vehicle observing the general condition of the paintwork and the body panels. As you move around the vehicle, note any blemishes on the paintwork and any areas of corrosion or damage on the bodywork. Remember that the only off-the-shelf replacement external panels, apart from a very limited number of new old stock panels, are the front and rear wings for all models. For all other parts, eg doors, bonnet, boot lid and valences, you will have to rely on good second-hand replacement parts, or employ the services of a specialist to weld in repair panels.

Front panels

Check for structural damage to the grille itself. The 'cheesegrater' grille fitted to 1952-1954 models is difficult to repair. Morris 1000 horizontal bars are more readily available if they need to be replaced. The bottom edge of the grille beneath the line of the bumper tends to rot out.

Bonnet and panel alignment – important.

Front wings

Check to see if they are metal or glassfibre. A quick tap will help distinguish which is fitted. Fixing glassfibre rear wings to Traveller models is a popular option. Look for signs of rust on the wing just above the headlamp rim, and for bubbling on the back edge of the wing where it meets the door.

Front doors

Look for signs of serious corrosion on the bottom edge of the doors, caused mainly by blocked drain holes over a long period of time. Even signs of bubbling on the paintwork in this area can be indicative of future problems and expense. Opening the door will allow for the bottom inside edge to be examined. Press firmly upwards and feel for flaking, rusty metal or worse still, a gaping hole all the way along.

Rear quarter panel

On 2-door Saloons and Convertible models, close attention should be paid to the curved area at the bottom of this panel. Distortion on the front edge may indicate previous repairs. Your magnet may come in handy here.

Later lamp bases are now available in ABS plastic!

Wings are prone to rust around the top of the headlamps. Heritage replacement wings are still available.

Rear wings

The area between the rear wings and the main body of the vehicle is prone to corrosion. The inner edge on the bottom of the rear wing is prone to splitting.

Boot area

Make a visual check of the bottom edge of the boot (trunk) lid. Those fitted to later models, which have an adhesive-fixed seal on the inside, rot quite badly. The alternative is to find a good second-hand replacement or commission a repair panel to be welded in.

Structural checks

The most important part of any appraisal of a Morris Minor.

Internal structural checks

A thorough check of the inside floor area is a definite prerequisite before purchase. Starting at the front of the vehicle, ease back the carpet that covers the inner sill, from the point where it reaches the floor. Check the edge of the floor where it meets the sill. If the carpet and the underfelt is wet, beware, there could be trouble ahead. Press hard all the way along the inner sill, squeezing it with both hands. If there are signs of weakness or movement then repairs – including new sills or floor panels – may be necessary.

Centre crossmember

This is the most critical area to check. Tip or fold forward the front seats. Lift the carpets to expose the floor area beneath the seats. The raised area running across the car is the top edge of the centre crossmember. Look for signs of corrosion or previous repair. If serious corrosion exists, note this as a possible reason to walk away. Full crossmember or crossmember ends are available but fitting them is a labour-intensive task.

Rear floor area

Continue checks to the inner sills and the seat belt mounting points on later cars. Examine carefully the floor area in both rear corners. The area beneath is adjacent to the front mounting point for the rear springs and, as such, is prone to metal fatigue.

Inside boot area

On opening the boot, examine the tops of the inner wings, noting the presence of original cage nuts for the fitting of the wings, as well as any corrosion or swelling of the metal. In the spare wheel compartment, look carefully in both rear corners. A torch will be useful here. This is a common area for repair and is often covered in thick underseal. Your probe may come in handy at this point. This area is next to the rear spring hanger mounting point where repairs are frequently required. It is also an area where water seeps in.

Engine bay
Checkpoints here include:
- The battery tray, the base of which may have been weakened by acid spills.
- The top edge of the inner wings, especially in the corners near the bulkhead.
- The 'tie plates', the panels with the big holes, in the base of the engine bay and the front crossmember panel which runs underneath the radiator.

The good news is that all these panels are available as remanufactured replacements.

Structural checks underside
In an ideal world, these checks should be made when the vehicle is on a ramp. The local MoT station might oblige if the owner is in agreement. If the owner has a garage with a pit in it, then with the benefit of a good torch, lead or inspection lamp, a thorough examination can be undertaken. Look out for the following key areas:

Front chassis legs
These run parallel each side of the engine. They are often weakened and distorted by being used as jacking points. Look for signs of welded patches. These items can look good but looks can be deceptive. Check for the soundness of the metal by tapping firmly with the handle of your screwdriver/probe. A clear pinging sound denotes sound metal, whereas a dull thud may indicate the presence of filler or weakened metal.

Outer sills
These run all the way along the outer edge of the floor area. Look for rusty areas of weakness in the area directly beneath the front doors. A boxing plate, which gives added strength to the body, is concealed beneath the door kick plate. If there are serious signs of corrosion on the bottom of the sills then the chances are that the boxing plate will have rusted through, too. On Convertible models, this is a critical area, as the boxing plate has double strength to compensate for the absence of a roof. Needless to say, if the sills are weak the car will start to fold in the middle. Door alignment will also be compromised. By looking at the bottom of the inner wings, front and rear, you may see further evidence of corrosion or previous attempts at repair.

Crossmember
Give serious consideration to the condition of the crossmember. Check for deterioration of the metal on the

Check condition of jacking points and sills.

Early style chassis plate with patent plate above located on bulkhead.

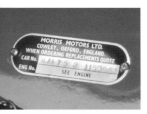

Later style chassis plate.

bottom edge, for the presence of jacking points on the end of the crossmember, and for signs of corrosion along its length where it meets the floor.

Spring hanger mounting points

Check the area where these meet the body. Look for areas of weakness, metal fatigue, or signs of previous repairs.

If, having carried out all these checks you discover that a considerable number of problems exist, it may well be time to consider walking away. If you feel that they are capable of repair and doing so is an option, then you may wish to use their existence as a bargaining point, having considered the rest of the vehicle.

Interior

Interior fittings and the dashboard layout will vary greatly from model to model. As mentioned previously, it will pay dividends to investigate the specifications of the model you are going to view, particularly if originality is high on your list of priorities.

On early models with a board headlining, pay particular attention to the rexine covering. This is virtually impossible to replace, so what you see is pretty much what you will get. On later models, check the headlining for rips, tears and original fit. If there are creases, lack of tension and general untidiness, then someone has probably tried to fit a replacement – not the easiest of jobs. Replacement headlinings are readily available for Saloon and Traveller models.

Seating is a priority. Checks on match, wear and tear and condition of the front seats are all prerequisites to giving the thumbs up. Seat webbing, replacement covers, matching trim and door cards are all available for the entire Morris Minor range. However, with four different types of interior fitted in the period 1956-1971, it is advisable to enquire whether the interior has been changed or updated. If in doubt, make enquires from other owners, or contact an owners club for advice.

Carpet sets are also obtainable for all models. For early Traveller models, the original rubber floor coverings are like the proverbial 'hens' teeth'. You are more likely to find a carpet set fitted.

Elsewhere, take note of any obtrusive modifications to the dash layout in terms of switches, accessories and gauges. Look to see if the indicator system has been changed to augment the use of semaphore indicators. Sometimes the unwanted holes have been drilled in inappropriate places, which can then detract from the appearance of the dash layout once they are removed. Additional work to rectify and repaint can be costly.

Finally, if the interior fittings have been updated by adding more comfortable modern seating, check to see the impact on the original bodywork of the vehicle. Remember to ask if the original seats and other original parts, such as indicator switches and the steering wheel, still exist, and whether they are available to you as part of the deal if you decide to purchase the car.

Mechanical

The A-Series engines fitted to the Morris Minor are well-known for being robust, dependable units. Nevertheless, they are fallible and problems can occur. The 803cc engine, as fitted to all models from 1952-1956, is the weakest of all the engines in terms of performance, and does suffer with a problem associated with burning out exhaust valves, particularly between the middle two cylinders. A symptom to look out for associated with this problem is unevenness when the engine is idling. It is not uncommon to find that 803cc engines have been replaced by later 948cc or 1098cc units.

Engine number is located on the engine block – adjacent to the dynamo-mounted coil.

All three engines have a problem with noisy timing chains. The cause is down to the fact that after a period of time the chains become stretched and are then noisy in operation. The noise is concentrated at the front of the engine. It is not a major task to have the timing chain replaced, and in the short term, it is not detrimental to the engine itself.

When examining the engine, some basic checks are necessary. Remove the oil filler cap and check for signs of a white mayonnaise-type deposit inside it. This may be a symptom of a leaking head gasket. Check the condition of the oil by removing the dipstick. Also look carefully for signs of oil leaks. These are all telltale signs as to the general state of the engine and how it has been maintained.

Starting the engine from cold can also give further clues to its condition. Morris Minors are renowned for starting on the first turn of the key. Check for this, as well as the smooth running of the engine when idling, after the choke has been pushed in. Listen for any nasty-sounding bottom end rumbles. It could be the big ends. Repetitive top end tapping noises could be tappets or worn valve gear, and a noisy or blowing exhaust could be a loose manifold or down pipe. While dealing with the exhaust, check for signs of excessive blue smoke; an indication of worn piston rings, or black smoke, too rich a mixture.

At this stage, it is possible to carry out some preliminary checks on other key components from the driver's seat while stationary. Check the clutch pedal pressure at the same time noting the ease with which the gears can be selected. Assess the operation of the handbrake, noting if it takes any more than five clicks to tension it fully. Finally, turn the steering wheel, noting any excessive play.

Turn the wheels outwards and then, moving to the front, check the front suspension components. Look for the rubber bushes on the lower arms to see if they are perished or well worn. Note any visible signs of greasing on the top links. Finally, exert firm downward pressure on the top of all wings and check for the number of bounces as the suspension settles. Any more than 1½ and the dampers will need replacing.

Are you still interested after all this? If so, look at the key points in Chapter 8 and then proceed to the more in-depth examination using the checklist and scoring system supplied in Chapter 9.

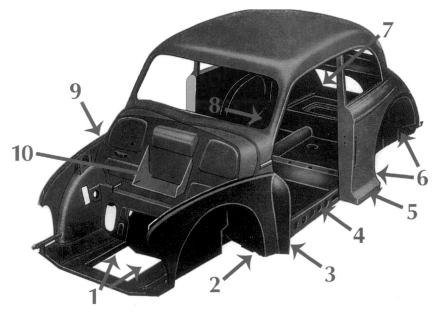

Ten key check points for rust and corrosion. 1. Front chassis legs. 2. Bottom of front inner wing. 3. Normally concealed door hinge pillar. 4. Inner and outer sills. 5. Bottom of rear quarter panel. 6. Front and rear spring hanger mounting points. 7. Rear boot floor corners. 8. Inner floor edges and central crossmember. 9. Inner wing top edge and corners. 10. Battery tray.

Check wings for evidence of accident damage, repairs or rusting. Pay attention to the area around the headlights and the rear edge of the wings for signs of bubbling.

Check alignment of the hood frame, condition of the fabric and door gaps. Do they taper?

Check front doors for signs of splitting near the quarter light, and excessive rot on the bottom edges.

Problems are often concealed behind other panels. Sill (rocker) finishers are a prime example. What horrors await?

Lighting, including amendments and upgrades, needs to be fully checked for efficiency, safety and appearance.

Traveller wood. Look for signs of soft spots in the wood, discolouration around the joints and ill-fitting rear doors.

Chrome items deteriorate badly. Replacements parts are available but cost can mount up quite quickly.

Interior seating. A huge range of different trim options were available. Check for damage, sagging seats and damp floor coverings.

Engine. Original specification or upgraded engine? Unleaded cylinder head?

Make thorough checks in the engine bay. Check for water and oil leaks and excessive oil spray. Examine the condition of hoses, clips and wiring.

Lift carpets and check the inner floor area for signs of damp, rust and metal fatigue.

9 Serious evaluation
– 60 minutes for years of enjoyment

Exterior
Paint

Ex	Gd	Av	Po
4	3	2	1

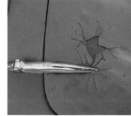

Original or resprayed? Identifying whether a Morris Minor has been the subject of a full or partial respray is relatively straightforward, due in part to its design, curved panels and the way it was assembled when new. External hinges, wing piping, detachable bonnet mouldings and an abundance of rubber seals, all make life difficult for the painter unless the vehicle is completely stripped down and subjected to a full bare metal respray. Getting an even paint finish on any Morris Minor is an art in itself.

Paint problems can be expensive to repair... and indicative of previous poor workmanship.

Telltale signs of substandard paintwork are easy to spot once you know where to look. One of the key areas of inspection is the rear wing piping, which, if unpainted, will be a slightly different shade and not as glossy as the adjacent paint. If paint is flaking off the plastic piping, this is a dead giveaway that the vehicle has been resprayed. Other items that will give an indication of the quality of the respray include the thin rubber seal at the base of the quarter light in the front doors, which invariably gets missed whilst masking, as well as the windscreen and rear screen rubbers which are often left in situ while painting is in progress. A ridge of flaking paint soon emerges. On Traveller models, the rubber joining strip between the cab roof and aluminium rear roof panel is another key area to check, as is the area around the factory-fitted windscreen washer jets on the later cars. Failure to remove these items prior to painting inevitably results in a build-up of paint around the bases.

If there are no signs of paint on any of the rubber seals and you have examined all of the areas above, then you are probably looking at a Minor that still has its original paintwork, or been subject to a labour-intensive bare metal paint job. If it is the latter, the vendor may have photographic evidence to back this up. If, however, the vehicle is sporting its original factory finish, the chances are it will be suffering from problems such as fading, oxidisation, micro blistering and bubbling, which are covered in Chapter 14.

If the paint job is relatively new, be cautious, it could be hiding a multitude of problems. Use your magnet to check for signs of the dreaded filler. Also look along the panels for signs of rippling and uneven surfaces.

If you are really serious about originality with regard to original colour and colour match, compare the exterior finish to that on the metal dash and in more inaccessible places where light may not have caused fading. Areas include the front scuttle below the parcel shelf, the area adjacent to trim panels in the front footwells or behind the door cards.

Details of shade authenticity is a matter of personal choice, unless of course you have aspirations of concours competition.

Panels

In this section we will revisit the areas already identified in Chapter 7; the aim being to look more closely, and then to objectively grade the various components.

External panels

This section covers the panels you can see without opening the bonnet (hood) or the boot (trunk).

On Saloon models, it is unusual to find much wrong with the roof, although occasionally there may be some signs of corrosion on the moulding where the roof joins the body of the car near the rear window. The rear section of the Traveller roof panel is aluminium and more vulnerable to dents. These can prove difficult to repair.

Front and rear wings should be carefully assessed. On front wings, take note of the areas around the headlights and the rear edge. Replacements are readily available but budget for ⬤ x400 before painting and fitting if you have to replace all four. Front doors are a major item to consider. Check the outer metal edge immediately beneath the quarter light for signs of splitting. Confirm the extent by checking the corresponding inner edge. This is a common fault. Welded repairs are possible. The bottom edge of all doors is a key area to check. If there are signs of bubbling or rust and the underside of the door has holes in it, then a second-hand replacement will be needed or a repair panel welded in. This will require expertise, as the door will need to be braced while the repair is carried out, so as to avoid distortion.

Final external panels to be assessed include the bonnet, boot, front panels and valences. All are prone to rust on bottom edges. Check the strength of the metal using a probe if necessary, but do not apply too much pressure for fear of causing further damage.

Traveller models

Traveller models require some specific attention when it comes to assessing the external panels. In addition to all of the above checks, note should be taken of the side and rear door panels. These are all aluminium and usually in good condition: however, on some older vehicles, the aluminium at the outer edges of the panels has begun to deteriorate and become crumbly. A warning sign that this might be occurring is the presence of bubbling on the edges of the paintwork. New aluminium panels can be cut to size and fitted quite easily. They are simply screwed to the wooden framework.

Wood frame

The wood frame on Traveller models should be subjected to rigorous examination. It is a structural part of the vehicle and is a MoT point. Critical areas to investigate are the top corners on the rear pillars. Discolouration, softness in the wood, or evidence of rotting

Traveller wood. Crucial MoT point (UK) so worthy of serious consideration.

wood and missing pieces should set alarm bells ringing. If this is accompanied by similar evidence elsewhere (such as the joints between the rear pillar and the main central timber on the three piece wheelarch panel, or the quarter panel footer), then start budgeting for replacement of some or all of the woodwork. Be wary of bodged repairs, and be very cautious indeed if you come across a Traveller with its wood painted (this is a possible walk away scenario unless the rest of the vehicle is exceptional). Rear doors should also be examined for deterioration of the wood. However, the external hinges need to be checked for rust, as well as wear. Rear door shutability on Travellers is a common problem. Too much play and they rattle, too tight a fit (possibly because of new door seals), and they do not shut flush with each other.

Shut lines. Panel alignment is all important, but sometimes difficult to achieve.

Shut lines

Ex Gd Av Po

Shut lines should be evenly spaced and consistent all around the vehicle. Key areas to examine are the bonnet and boot. They are often out of alignment but usually capable of being adjusted. However, poor or uneven shut lines can signal other more serious problems. If considerable welding repairs have been carried out on the vehicle, then it could be that the main structure of the vehicle is slightly out of alignment. Poor bonnet alignment can result from repairs to inner wing panels that are not aligned properly.

The critical area to view on a Morris Minor is the door shut lines in the A- and B-post areas. If the shut lines are not consistent, there could be a number of reasons for it. The door hinges could be worn and the door has dropped, the A-post supporting the door has rotted out at its obscured bottom edge, or the vehicle has not been sufficiently braced when previous welding repairs have taken place. In the case of the A-post rotting out, a simple check is to take a firm grip of the door and lift it firmly upwards. If you see flexing in the pillar where the door hinges are, that is evidence of poor alignment and an indication of further work.

Another more simple reason for poor door alignment is the inaccurate positioning of the door catch mechanisms. These are capable of adjustment but are often not set up properly, giving rise to difficulties when trying to shut the door.

Convertible models

Ex Gd Av Po

Door alignment is also critical on Convertible models. The absence of a roof, though compensated by additional strengthening panels in the sill area, means that there is more flexibility within the body structure of these models. It is said that if you park with one wheel on the pavement that you may not be able to get out of the car by opening the door, such is the degree of flexibility. Tapering gaps between the top of the window frame, the top of the rear side window and the bottom of the door, could indicate possible structural weakness.

Exterior trim

Bumper blades, badges, 2-door door handles, as well as bonnet and boot hinges, are readily available from specialist suppliers. Apart from the bumper blades, all other items are produced using mazak or 'monkey metal'. Over time, this has a tendency to pit badly and is difficult to replate/rechrome. Consequently, new replacement parts are necessary.

Morris 1000 parts are more readily available than those for earlier Series II models. Rare items include the chrome split windscreen inserts which are chrome on brass, and although flimsy, can be replated. Other rarities include rear boot badges that have a reflector fitted, and rear boot hinges which have a different profile to later 1000 items.

Wipers

Ex 4 Gd 3 Av 2 Po 1

Wiper arms and blades are quite different in terms of design across the model range. Arms and blades can be accessed fairly easily, though the early Series II items are the province of autojumbles and owners club sources.

Soft Top

Ex 4 Gd 3 Av 2 Po 1

Convertible hoods and hood frames are different in terms of design and pattern for Series II and Morris 1000 models. Rear window size varies, with a small celluloid panel being a feature of the canvas and mohair hoods originally fitted to the early cars (1953-1956). Plastic PVC hoods with a much larger rear screen were characteristic of the Morris 1000 models (1956-1969). These were available in a variety of colours to complement the trim. Availability is good with a number of specialist companies offering a custom-made fitting service. A hood bag is not always available, as some owners seem to regard it as an optional extra.

Glass

Ex 4 Gd 3 Av 2 Po 1

It's worth checking whether the glass components have been security marked. Provided this is not too unsightly, it can be an asset. Screen availability for Morris 1000 models is excellent. However, for split screen models, the situation is quite different. The flat panels are sometimes badly scratched which can be a problem when driving in bright sunlight. It is possible to commission replacement screens.

Lights

Ex 4 Gd 3 Av 2 Po 1

Availability of replacement light units is generally good, although very early rear light bases, complete with red glass,

Badging varied slightly throughout the model range. Early Series II had boot badge with reflector.

Three types of wiper systems were adopted.

Later 1000 large window. Hood frames and rear window aperture differed from Series II to Morris 1000.

are the province of autojumbles and firms specialising in lighting for older vehicles. They were used by other marques, including MG, so prices can be high.

Later Morris 1000 rear light bases were originally made of mazak. Consequently they can pit badly. New units, virtually indistinguishable from the original, but made of ABS plastic, are readily available. Semaphore indicators continued in use until 1961, and for a time, an interim arrangement which provided for flashing indication with a combined red brake/indicator at the rear and white sidelights at the front, was used. Though perfectly legal, it confuses MoT testers who want to see orange. It's usually the owners who see red!!

It is commonplace to find additions to the original lighting arrangement on vehicles manufactured between 1952-1963. If originality or concours is a major consideration, check out carefully the location of extra lights and indicators. Look for fixings to the bodywork and check the location and condition of any additional switches and associated wiring.

Early Series II glass rear lights (rare).

948cc Morris 1000 rear lights.

1098cc Morris 1000 combined indicator/brake light.

Wheels and tyres

Ex	Gd	Av	Po
4	3	2	1

14in wheels were fitted to all models. However, the type of wheel and method of fixing varied. Early Series II wheels had a bolt type fixing and three locating pins for attaching hubcaps. With the introduction of the A-Series rear axle from January 1954, new stronger wheels with different dimensions were fitted. This rendered them incompatible with earlier models.

All these wheels were prone to splitting around the fixing points, something worth checking with the hubcaps removed. Recognition of this problem saw the introduction of a stronger wheel with raised mouldings for the location of hubcaps and no brake-adjusting hole. Morris 1000 wheels carried this style forward.

Series II wheels tended to be painted body colour. 948cc models on the other hand had a variety of colour schemes. Dark Green, Turquoise and Black vehicles had Birch Grey wheels until 1959, when Pearl Grey wheels were introduced. Late 948cc and 1098cc models had wheels finished in Old English White, but from 1967, Silver was used.

All Morris Minors were supplied with 5.20x14 crossply tyres originally. Dunlop C41 tyres were fitted initially, but this designation was later changed to D75. Commercial vehicles had wider wheels and it is commonplace to find these fitted to Saloons, Travellers and Convertibles, along with radial tyres.

Later wheels had moulded shape and fixings.

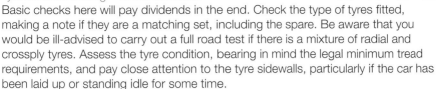

Basic checks here will pay dividends in the end. Check the type of tyres fitted, making a note if they are a matching set, including the spare. Be aware that you would be ill-advised to carry out a full road test if there is a mixture of radial and crossply tyres. Assess the tyre condition, bearing in mind the legal minimum tread requirements, and pay close attention to the tyre sidewalls, particularly if the car has been laid up or standing idle for some time.

Wheels should be checked for signs of kerb damage, and early wheels for excessive wear and possible splitting around the bolt/stud holes. The very early wheels have a tendency to buckle. Evidence of excessive rusting or pitting, particularly on later wheels, should be noted, as restoring to factory standard may prove difficult. Be reassured; good replacement second-hand wheels are still plentiful through club sources and autojumbles, though the much sought-after wider van and pick-up wheels may take some finding.

Duo tone interior with complementary carpets. Lift carpets to check structural nature of floors.

Interior
Carpets/floor coverings

Whilst it is important to check the condition for the reasons mentioned in Chapter 7, it is reassuring to know that replacement carpet sets are available for all models. Differing patterns, to take account of the positioning of the gear lever, are available. It is no longer possible to obtain the original 'Karvel' material as used on early models, but good quality substitutes with authentic colour matching are available.

Original rubber floor coverings, as fitted to Traveller models, are highly prized and much sought-after. If available, regard this as a major plus point.

Late Series II 4-door Saloon interior. Just as it came out of the showroom!

Headling

Board headlinings, as fitted to the early Series II models, need to be carefully appraised for condition, shape and fit. Some distortion can occur due to damp, particularly in the panel which fits beneath the rear window. Checking the condition of the irreplaceable rexine covering should be a priority. For later models with a one-piece tensioned headlining, it's a matter of assessing the relative merits of the fit and condition of an original headlining versus that of a replacement. Plus points include having replacement items available, but the downside is that for the home restorer, it is a daunting task to tackle.

Check headlining for fit and originality.

Door cards have a tendency to warp if wet!

Door cards

Door cards on the Morris Minor are of simple construction. The many varied coverings, allied to the rest of the trim, are normally in good or sound condition. The main problem rests with the bottom of the door cards on the front doors. The hardboard absorbs water, becomes distorted, and the adhesive ceases to hold the covering in place. Repairs are possible, and for later Morris 1000 models all components are available to match the corresponding seat coverings.

Door locks

Door locks do not feature highly in the list of the Morris Minor's strongest points. By now, most of the locks are well worn. The external lock was only fitted to the driver's door. However, there is a locking catch on the inside edge of the passenger door. Check to see if this is present and operative. Other internal locks are operated by

4-door door handles – hard to find. New old stock mostly.

pushing the internal handle forward (4-door Saloons). Such was the disregard for locks, that LHD models did not have an external lock on the corresponding drivers door until the mid-1960s. Car security can be compromised if the quarter light catch is broken. Check to see if any additional security has been added. For example, cut-out switches, alarm systems or other anti-theft devices.

Door handles

Strong and robust, there is little to fault the external or internal door handles. Excessive wear, easily identified by vertical movement of the handle, could signal future failure. Unsightly corrosion on the surface of the external handles is the only other drawback.

Internal handles and window winders – robust.

Window winders

Strong, robust and functional, the window winders are rarely a problem. However, in the event of the window winding mechanism failing, it is a major undertaking to strip the door in order to repair or replace it.

Steering wheel

Steering wheels changed on three occasions during 1952-1971. Early models had Bakelite steering wheels with three sets of four-wire spokes. These are much sought-after in sound original condition. They have a tendency to crack, and in extreme circumstances can disintegrate, leaving a sticky residue. If this gets on to the front seats of the vehicle, it will damage the leather or vynide facings.

803cc early dash, Bakelite steering wheel. Note floor covering.

The dished steering wheel, as fitted to the early Morris 1000 models (which also had three four-wired spokes), is more common, and although prone to cracking, is more readily

Combination cluster of warning lights on central speedometer.

Circulatory heaters were an optional extra for a long time on standard models.

available should one need replacing. The centre boss on these models was purely decorative, as the horn push was on the end of the indicator stalk.

The later two-spoke steering wheel, as fitted to later 1000s, is the most easily sourced type. It reverted to having a horn push fitted to the centre. It is quite strong and less liable to crack. Check the area where the spokes meet the rim … just in case.

Instrument panel

Simplicity is the characteristic feature of all the instrument panels fitted to the Morris Minor. Early models featured a distinctive gold coloured dash which had the instrument cluster in front of the driver. Speedometer, fuel and oil pressure gauges completed the line up. Consequently, it is common to find additional gauges fitted. Provided these are not too obtrusive and do not detract from the symmetry of the dash layout, consider them a functional asset.

All other models have a central speedometer and, depending on which model you are viewing, it may have a different coloured face. Bronze faced speedometers were characteristic of the later Series II and 948cc Morris 1000 models. These incorporated a fuel gauge and had four warning lights for oil pressure, indicator illumination, main beam and ignition. Later Morris 1000 models had black faced speedometers with similar warning lights, albeit in different positions.

Check the condition of the surrounding paintwork on the dash panel, and the fitment of additional gauges and switches.

948cc dished steering wheel.

1098cc dash plus two-spoke steering wheel.

Dash mounted ignition warning light on early Series II.

Handbrake (parking brake)

Check for condition and ease of operation. Three types were fitted. In early models, a substantial gold coloured handbrake, with a top edge release mechanism, operated the cables that were linked to the rear brake shoes. On Morris 1000 models, a button release version was used on a much more compact handbrake. Early versions had a chromed release button, but later models sported a cheaper plastic version. On occasions, the spring-loaded release button has been known to shoot the entire contents out of the end. Finding the components can be fun!

In terms of operation and adjustment, any more than four or five clicks probably means that adjustment is needed. Cable adjustment is via nuts on the end of the cables on the interior of the vehicle next to the handbrake lever.

Boot area. Prone to damp ... and rust.

Roomy Traveller showing maximum load space.

Boot (trunk) interior

Ex [4] Gd [3] Av [2] Po [1]

The boot area on Saloon and Convertible models is very spartan. Concentrate on structural items here as there really is only the plain black wooden boot floor panels to see. As mentioned previously, check the exposed inner wings for signs of corrosion and ensure that the original caged nuts are visible.

Spare wheel area.

Spare wheel compartment
Ex [4] Gd [3] Av [2] Po [1]

The spare wheel compartment is situated beneath the boot floor. Your torch will be required here. With the spare wheel removed, check the flange around the petrol tank for signs of swollen metal. Also make a thorough check of each corner, taking note of any previous repairs. Any signs of excessive underseal should be treated with suspicion, as should evidence of water ingress. This part of the vehicle is often neglected. A case of out of sight, out of mind.

Traveller spare wheel compartment – neatly concealed.

Tool kit. Functional but dated. Note starting handle.

Tool kit
Ex [4] Gd [3] Av [2] Po [1]

It is unusual to find a complete tool kit with early vehicles as these included a host of items, including a wheel pump, grease gun, box spanners, feeler gauges, screw type jack, hub cap remover and wheel brace. All were stored in a wraparound plastic tool roll. By the time the last Series of vehicles was supplied, the tool kit was very minimalist, consisting only of a hub cap remover, wheel brace and jack and small grease gun. These items were wrapped in a black plastic tool roll.

Mechanicals
Under the bonnet (hood)
Ex [4] Gd [3] Av [2] Po [1]

With it released, open the bonnet, noting whether the catch is broken: first impressions are important here. The spacious area around the engine will enable you to make a visual check of the inner wings, bulkhead and engine bay floor. Note the extent of any rust and any previous repairs.

A clean engine bay, provided it is consistent with the rest of the car, may be a positive sign that the vehicle has been well maintained. This might be a time to enquire about service history. Look for any stickers that might indicate recent oil changes or the date of the next MoT.

If, following the fifteen minute evaluation, you have not yet ascertained whether the correct type of engine is fitted, now is the time to ask or check.

Subtly check to see if the engine is still warm while running your eye over the components you are about to check in more detail. Are there signs of neglect? Are the fluid levels correct in the battery, the engine and the radiator? (Only check the radiator if the engine is cold, for fear of scalding.) Are there any visible oil or water leaks, which may be worthy of further investigation?

Engine and chassis numbers

Ex [4] Gd [3] Av [2] Po [1]

Chassis numbers are more important than engine numbers when it comes to confirming the authenticity of any Morris Minor. Of course, it is a bonus if the original engine is still in use and all the numbers match. Details of chassis number prefixes and their interpretation are in Chapter 17. It is usually fairly straightforward to check these out, provided the relevant identification plates are on the bulkhead and the engine, and the relevant V5C document is available. This is particularly relevant when checking the authenticity of a genuine Convertible model. The prefix for Saloons should be compared with that for Convertibles (MA2S for later Saloons as opposed to MAT for Convertibles). This is not always foolproof, as certain unscrupulous people switch chassis plates. Other checks are outlined elsewhere.

**803cc A-Series.
Courtesy of Austin
Motor Company.
Mated with a weak
gearbox.**

Radiator and fans

Ex [4] Gd [3] Av [2] Po [1]

With the engine switched off, check for signs of leakage, particularly along the edge which runs beneath the header tank.

Look carefully to see if there are any signs of damage to the vertical cores immediately in front of the fan blade, and make a visual check in the area immediately beneath the radiator for signs of wet or dry brown deposits. This could indicate recent problems and the presence of sludge in the system. On early models, look for the radiator drain tap at the bottom, and without using undue force, check if it will turn. Failure to do so may indicate lack of maintenance. Provided it is safe to do so, remove the radiator cap and inspect the water level and colour. Is antifreeze present and the liquid clear? Any other scenario may be bad news, particularly if there is an oily deposit present. Check fan blades for signs of damage.

**948cc A-Series.
Well sorted engine
and gearbox.**

**1098cc A-Series.
Best performance
– trusty unit.**

Hoses

Ex [4] Gd [3] Av [2] Po [1]

Signs of perished hoses, inadequately tightened jubilee clips, and indications of leakage, sometimes typified by crystallised antifreeze, are all further indications of a lack of regular maintenance. Those with an eye to originality should check if early Series II vehicles retain the use of canvas-covered fluted radiator hoses.

Wiring

Ex	Gd	Av	Po
4	3	2	1

The wiring on all Morris Minors is quite simplistic, both in terms of layout and design. Braided wiring looms were fitted to all models. Individual colour coded wires have an outer insulation coating which, over time, becomes brittle and therefore potentially dangerous. The wiring loom is most visible in the engine bay where it passes through the bulkhead.

Neat wiring showing regulator box and external fuses. Early Series II.

Areas worthy of checking include the wiring at the regulator box which is fitted in the engine bay, and the loom itself, particularly where it passes behind metal clips attached to the bodywork, and underneath the radiator. Beware of heavily taped looms, exposed wires and crumbling insulation. Pay particular attention to areas that have been subject to repair, particularly welded repairs, which may have inadvertently caused unwanted damage. Watch out for unsightly additions to the wiring with obtrusive snap connectors, and check for any signs of corrosion on connectors.

Battery

Ex	Gd	Av	Po
4	3	2	1

Fitting wiring loom. Cotton braided looms were used originally and are still available.

The battery is located in the engine bay, just above the engine in a special tray that incorporates locating points for the retaining bar. The 12V positive earth electrical system relied on a succession of large batteries during the time the vehicles were in production. Large rubber cased black batteries are available from specialist suppliers and are favoured by collectors and concours exhibitors. For daily drivers, just about any battery will do. It is wise to note the fitment, general condition – including the state and type of terminals fitted – the fluid level and polarity. It's worth confirming this, as it is possible this may have been reversed to accommodate the fitting of aftermarket accessories.

Simple washer system – an aftermarket accessory.

Windscreen washer system

Ex	Gd	Av	Po
4	3	2	1

Pre-1961 windscreen washers were not fitted as standard. Subsequent MoT requirements meant that they had to be fitted retrospectively. Consequently, non-standard and sometimes very obtrusive systems are fitted. Check for method of operation and efficiency. Most of the water containers are fitted in the engine bay.

Engine leaks

Ex	Gd	Av	Po
4	3	2	1

The A-Series engine has a number of areas which are prone to oil leaks. These can be more inconvenient rather than damaging, unless of course the lost oil is not replaced. At the top end of the engine, the main problem relates to the rocker cover gasket. Seepage here, though unsightly, can be easily solved by fitting a new cork gasket. More difficult is the joint between the cylinder head and the engine block. Leakage here will require removal of the cylinder head in order for repairs to be made. Leaks of a different kind may also be observed to the rear of the engine where a heater tap is positioned, particularly when in the 'off' position. Other engine leaks are considered elsewhere under 'ramp check'.

Ex	Gd	Av	Po
4	3	2	1

Engine mountings

The front engine mountings are easily spotted on the two mounting turrets each side of the engine. The condition of the rubber mountings should be checked for signs of wear and deterioration. The rear gearbox mounting rubbers, located on the gearbox crossmember, are best checked when the car is on a ramp. Of equal importance is the engine steady bar which is fitted between the rear of the engine and the bulkhead. The rubber spacers should be checked for signs of excessive wear.

Ex	Gd	Av	Po
4	3	2	1

Exhaust manifold and downpipes

Problems are rare where these items are concerned, but sounds of the exhaust blowing may be detected when the engine is idling if either the manifold or downpipe is loose.

Ex	Gd	Av	Po
4	3	2	1

Core plugs

The three main circular core plugs, found on the side of the engine block, tend to rust from the inside. Signs that this may be happening can be detected by rust staining on the engine casing.

Ex	Gd	Av	Po
4	3	2	1

Brake master cylinder

Located in the driver's side front chassis leg, the brake master cylinder tends to get neglected. Once you have found it, check the fluid level and note signs of recent attention. It's a swine to replace, but parts are available.

Early type brake cylinders as used on Series II models.

Clutch mechanism

Mechanical Borg and Beck clutch capable of manual adjustment. Assess operation on test drive.

Ex	Gd	Av	Po
4	3	2	1

Carburettor/fuel pump

Practical, straightforward, single SU type carburettor used in conjunction with SU fuel pump, noted for its characteristic ticking when ignition is switched on or fuel is low. Problems, if they do arise, usually centre on needle adjustment or replacement. Routine checks on the dash pot, which should be topped up with light engine oil, should be made.

Parts for brakes and suspension are readily available for all models.

Steering rack

Positive, direct steering is almost a given with a Morris Minor, courtesy of the rack and pinion system. Check it out on test and make a note to look for splits on the rubber gaiters each end of the rack, and any obvious signs of fluid leakage when doing a ramp check.

Front hub bearings and steering joints

Serious checks here are best completed when the vehicle is safely jacked up and it is possible to spin the wheel and listen for ominous rumbling noises. Front wheel bearings can be adjusted using the centre nut, but if this does not cure the problem, replacement is the only answer. It's best to replace both bearings at the same time. Steering arms do wear over time, as do the ball joints at the end of the steering rack.

Front suspension remained unchanged in basic design throughout production.

Front suspension

With the 'bounce' test already complete (Chapter 7), concentrate on the condition of the components which make up the front suspension. Look for worn or perished rubber components, signs of recent maintenance on the top links (trunnions), and pay particular attention to the eye bolt bushes. By using a large screwdriver, you can attempt to move the bottom suspension arm away from the bodywork. If there is movement then the eyebush will need replacing.

Front brakes

Visual checks here should centre on the general condition of the flexible brake hoses, the brake pipes themselves, including a note on whether copper type replacements have been fitted, and any obvious signs of brake fluid leakage. It's certainly worth noting if any nonstandard fitments have been added.

If only your would-be purchase looked like this! Note excellent crossmember.

Gearbox

Look to see if a standard specification engine and gearbox is fitted. Interchangeability is possible, but it is ill-advised to have a larger engine mated to a lower specification box. Assessment is best finalised after the test drive but make a visual check for oil leaks at this stage.

Rear suspension and brakes

The condition of the rear leaf springs, associated rubber components and Armstrong rear dampers should all be assessed for signs of perishing, leaks and damage. The individual leaf springs can break, but this is tough to spot on visual inspection. Revisit this area on the ramp inspection

Early Series II models shared all suspension, brake and axle parts with the Series MM model shown here.

when it may be easier to carry out essential checks on the condition of rear brake pipes, back plates and signs of leaking brake cylinders.

Rear axle

Ex	Gd	Av	Po
4	3	2	1

Anticipate some rear axle whine when you get to drive the vehicle; it is part of owning a Minor. Also enquire if the differential has been changed at any point. Various options were available as part of the original specification. It's worth asking if the half shafts have been changed or replaced. New stronger versions are now available as a post-production upgrade. Check for signs of oil seepage which is likely to stem from the differential oil seal.

Immaculate underside showing early Series II type rear axle.

Test drive

Ex	Gd	Av	Po
4	3	2	1

Are you sitting comfortably? Seat adjustment is not as straightforward as on a modern car. Check proximity to the controls, the angle of the seat and the support available. Note too the position of the pedal controls. Is it possible to press more than one at once? Are external mirrors fitted? Are they any use?

Cold start

Ex	Gd	Av	Po
4	3	2	1

Close pedal arrangement can take some getting used to.

Check choke adjustment. Key start or pull start? First time start is usual and the engine should idle quite happily provided it is not revving too high. With the choke fully pushed in, does the engine still run and has the ignition warning light gone out?

Ideally, your route should take in a variety of road conditions. Before setting off, it's worth reminding yourself that the Morris Minor does not have syncromesh on first gear.

Assess the ease with which you can use the clutch and select first gear. Is the clutch heavy to use? Is there excessive travel on the pedal? Is it difficult to select the gears? Check for the point of the bite on the clutch and prepare for lift off!

Points to consider here are whether there are any appreciable signs of judder as you set off. This could be indicative of a broken or badly adjusted engine steady bar or suspect engine mountings.

Gearbox operation.

Ex	Gd	Av	Po
4	3	2	1

You will quickly be able to assess the usability of the gearbox. When safe to do so, accelerate quickly in each gear, checking whether it jumps out of gear. Check too for clutch slip, denoted by increasing high revs without a corresponding increase in speed. Also check how smooth the car is when you reverse, particularly up a slight gradient.

Steering feel

Take note of the steering and assess how light and positive it is. Check for signs of pulling to the side. This could be influenced by tyre pressure, the camber of the road or a lack of balance in the wear and/or replacement of suspension components.

Noises

For one of the most distinctive noises associated with the Morris Minor, allow yourself the pleasure of decelerating on a downhill slope. The exhaust noise is sure to turn heads. However, listen for more ominous sounds or clunks, too. Rear axle whine varies in degree, as does wind noise. This can result from worn seals on the quarter light windows. With Convertible models, there is usually additional noise depending on the tautness of the hood when in the 'up' position. Wheel bearing noise will transmit through the car and will vary depending which way you are cornering. Listen for any uncharacteristic noises coming from the engine.

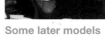

Performance

Take account of the expected performance for the model you are driving. Remember, in standard specification this is very modest by today's standards. However, be conscious of sluggish performance through the gears, a plateau in acceleration below that of what you would normally expect, as well as poor performance in handling or stopping. Signs such as these should, on your return, prompt further investigation into fuel mixture, braking efficiency and suspension weaknesses.

Some later models – 1970 onwards – were fitted with alternators.

Oil pressure

Where fitted, the oil pressure warning light becomes operative at 15psi. Stop and investigate if it becomes operative while driving.

Water temperature

82 degree centigrade thermostats were fitted to all the vehicles covered by this book. Take time to try out the heater controls and test their efficiency … if one is fitted! Pay particular attention to the effectiveness of recirculatory heaters fitted to early cars.

Boot area and fuel tank aperture.

Charging rate

It is worth checking if there has been an upgrade to fit an alternator to improve charging rate.

Instruments

Instrumentation is basic to say the least. Check operation

Inner floors and sills of Morris Minor's monocoque structure.

of standard equipment as well as any supplementary switches for lighting, screen washers or security.

Ramp check

Ex	Gd	Av	Po
4	3	2	1

Most items have already been mentioned, but if the opportunity is available to use the facility to view the underside, do not pass it up.

Starting from the rear of the vehicle, examine the fuel tank carefully for signs of weakness or perforation. Replacing the tank is expensive and repair is difficult.

Note all of the floor area, taking account of the following: the boot floor, especially the corners. The front and rear spring hanger mounting points and surrounding floor area. The full extent of the sills each side of the car. The crossmember, including the end where the jacking points should be. The front chassis legs each side of the engine. The tie plates and the critical points where the front suspension is attached to the body.

Note the extent of original rust-free metal, the extent of previously welded repairs, the use of replacement repair panels and, most importantly, the extent of any imminently required repairs.

Leak checks

Ex	Gd	Av	Po
4	3	2	1

Examine the following areas for signs of leaks which may necessitate oil seal replacement or new parts.

Rear axle, gearbox, shocker absorbers, rear engine seals, brake hoses, wheel cylinders and steering rack gaiters. Examine closely the fuel pipes and brake lines for corrosion.

Take note of the exhaust. Is it mild steel or stainless steel? Look on the passenger side front floor for the presence of a heat shield above the exhaust.

Rear dampers should be checked for leakage here.

Evaluation procedure

Add up the total points score:

228 = excellent, possibly concours; 171 = good; 114 = average; 57 = poor. Cars scoring over 160 should be completely usable, requiring only routine maintenance and care to be kept in good condition. Cars scoring between 57 and 115 will probably require a full restoration. Those scoring between 116 and 159 will need a very careful assessment of the work necessary, and its cost, in order to reach a realistic valuation.

10 Auctions
– sold! Another way to buy your dream

Auction pros & cons
Pros: Auctions are trade markets, so prices are lower and you could grab a bargain. Auctioneers usually guarantee ownership, and at the venue it should be possible to check all relevant paperwork and get 24 hours' warranty.

Cons: You normally only get limited information beforehand, and there's restricted scope to examine cars thoroughly. Cars are often not started and never road tested, so try to arrive early on preview day to see the lots being off-loaded. The cars often need valeting, which should not put you off.

Decide your personal limit and stick to it, including the buyer's premium – it's easy to overbid.

Catalogue prices and payment details
When you purchase the catalogue of the vehicles in the auction, it often acts as a ticket allowing two people to attend the viewing days and the auction. Catalogue details tend to be comparatively brief, but will include information such as 'one owner from new, low mileage, full service history', etc. It will also usually show you a guide price to give you some idea of what to expect to pay, and will tell you what is charged as a 'buyer's premium'. The catalogue will also contain details of acceptable forms of payment. An immediate part-payment or deposit is usually requested, with the balance payable within 24 hours. Check for cash and credit card limits, and options such as personal cheques/checks, debit cards or bank drafts. The car won't be released until paid for, with storage at your cost until completion.

Buyer's premium
A buyer's premium will be added to the hammer price: don't forget this in your calculations. It is not usual for there to be a further state tax or local tax on the purchase price and/or on the buyer's premium.

Viewing
In some instances it's possible to view the day before. Staff or owners may unlock doors, engine and luggage compartments for inspection, or start the engine. Crawling around the car is fine but you may not jack up a vehicle – hence your mirror.

Bidding
Before you take part in the auction, decide your maximum bid – and stick to it!

Lots are sold in numerical order so get to the sale room in good time. It may take a while for the auctioneer to reach the lot you are interested in, so use that time to observe how other bidders behave. A phrase such as 'It's with me at ...' means the car hasn't yet reached reserve. 'It's for sale at ...' means the car will now go to the highest bidder.

When it's the turn of your vehicle, attract the auctioneer's attention and make an early bid. The auctioneer will then look to you for a reaction every time another bid is made. Usually, the bids will be in fixed increments until bidding slows, when smaller increments will often be accepted before the hammer falls. If you want to withdraw from the bidding, make sure the auctioneer understands your intentions – a vigorous shake of the head when he or she looks at you for the next bid should do the trick.

Assuming that you are the successful bidder, the auctioneer will note your card or paddle number, and from that moment on you will be responsible for the vehicle.

If the vehicle is unsold, either because it failed to reach the reserve or because there was little interest, it may be possible to negotiate with the owner, via the auctioneers, after the sale is over.

eBay & the internet
eBay and other online auctions cover the best and the worst of the auction spectrum. It may be possible to bid across continents, but have a trusted person inspect the car and report back to you.

Most on-line sources show the seller's location, and may even allow you to search by distance from home, which can be useful. Always check, however, that the car is actually at the seller's location. It is usually best to choose your upper limit and bid that at the outset.

Remember too that it will be very difficult to obtain satisfaction if a dishonest seller disappears with your money, or a car doesn't arrive because it never existed.

Auctioneers
Barrett-Jackson www.barrett-jackson.com
Bonhams www.bonhams.com
British Car Auctions (BCA) www.bca-europe.com or www.british-car-auctions.co.uk
Cheffins www.cheffins.co.uk
Christies www.christies.com
Coys www.coys.co.uk
eBay www.ebay.com/www.ebay.co.uk
H&H www.classic-auctions.co.uk
RM www.rmauctions.com
Shannons www.shannons.com.au
Silver www.silverauctions.com

11 Paperwork

– correct documentation is essential!

The paper trail

The best Morris Minors usually come with a large portfolio of paperwork accumulated and passed on by a succession of owners. The documentation represents the real history of the car and from it can be deduced the care the vehicle has received, how much it's been used, which specialists have worked on it, and details of repairs and restorations. All of this information is priceless, so be very wary of Morris Minors with little paperwork.

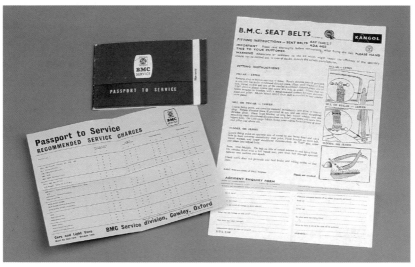

A fully documented history not only adds an interesting dimension to any potential purchase, it can also add value to the asking price.

Registration documents

All countries/states have some system of vehicle and/or ownership registration. Lack of ownership certification is normally a warning that something is not right.

Where documents exist, check they're originals and match the car. Sellers should issue a signed, dated and addressed receipt.

Remember that for foreign-registered cars, you, or the importer, will need to pay duty, and this, plus the title issues, takes time and effort to administer.

Roadworthiness certificate

Most administrations require that vehicles are regularly tested to prove that they are safe to use on the public highway. Tests are usually carried out at approved locations and old certificates can confirm the car's history. Ideally your candidate will be on the road, fully certified, permitting a proper test drive.

Road licence

The administration of every country/state charges some kind of tax for the use of its road system. The road 'licence', and how it is displayed, varies enormously.

Whatever its form, the road licence must relate to the vehicle carrying it, and must be present and valid if the vehicle is to be driven on the public highway. The value of the licence will depend on the length of time it's valid.

In the UK, if a vehicle is untaxed because it has not been used for a period of time, the owner has to inform the licensing authorities, otherwise the vehicle's date-related registration number will be lost and there will be a lot of paperwork to get it re-registered. Also in the UK, vehicles built before the end of 1972 are provided with tax discs free of charge, which must still be displayed. Car clubs can often provide formal proof that a particular car qualifies for this valuable concession.

Certificates of authenticity

Production records for Morris Minors are held at the Heritage Motor Museum, Gaydon, Warwickshire, England. It is possible to obtain a Heritage Certificate detailing production dates and specification for a fee. The Morris Minor Owners Club is also recognised as an authenticating body by the DVLA, for the purpose of retaining original registration numbers and for issuing dating certificates.

Valuation certificate

The seller may have a valuation certificate stating how much the car is worth. Such documents are usually needed for 'agreed value' insurance but should act only as confirmation of your own assessment, rather than a guarantee of value, because the expert has probably not even seen the car, only photos. See Chapter 16 for organizations providing valuations.

Service & restoration history

If the seller claims that the car has been restored, expect receipts and photographic evidence. If this includes engine work, take note of the rebuilder's name because if acknowledged experts have worked on the engine it's a hopeful sign. Make it a condition of purchase that you receive at least copies of photographs, if not originals.

Items like the original bill of sale, handbook, parts invoices and repair or parts bills all add to the story of the car. Even a correct brochure for the car's model year, or original contemporary road tests are useful documents.

12 What's it worth to you?
– let your head rule your heart!

Condition

If the car you have been looking at is really bad, by now you may already have given up and decided to look elsewhere. If you have used the marking system in Chapter 9, you will have a sound idea of which category the vehicle falls into. Excellent, maybe even concours, good, average or poor condition. It may even be a rare basket case with some intrinsic worth. You are now faced with the task of deciding what you are prepared to pay, and whether you are going to meet the vendor's asking price.

Deciding what is a fair price for the vehicle is a tough task if you are not familiar with the Morris Minor scene. Do not despair; help is at hand in the form of various price guides, which are regularly updated to take account of changing market values. Club publications, as well as a number of reputable classic car magazines, regularly produce comparative prices for different models, taking account of condition, rarity and roadworthiness. Seek out the most up-to-date prices you can. It is important to read any accompanying guidance notes before interpreting the actual prices.

Note that trends can change, too. Some years ago Convertible models were much sought-after and commanded top prices. At present Traveller models are in favour. Anticipating the next trend is anybody's guess as there are so many different models and engine types to choose from. This is an important consideration as the Condition 1 price can be a determining factor in purchasing decisions on less valuable cars. Paying a few hundred pounds for a mechanically sound vehicle requiring restoration may be worthwhile if the model is desirable, in short supply, and capable of realising most if not all of the costs when restored to excellent or concours standard. Equally, a similar, less desirable model incurring all the same restoration costs but with the potential to be worth only 50% as much may not be such a sound financial proposition.

Other key points relate to whether the purchase is as the result of a private sale, or from a dealer or an auction. The latter will carry dealer premiums and commission fees respectively. Generally speaking there is more scope for negotiation with a private sale.

Desirable options/extras

Factory fitted options were few and far between when the vehicles were in production. Heaters, extra sun visors and over-riders were just some of the items listed, all things you would expect

Owner-added items like this alternator can be beneficial.

Such personalised extras are not to everyone's taste.

Photographs taken throughout a restoration can be very helpful and reassuring.

as standard fitment now. Apart from something like an external metal sun visor, post-production items are more likely to have a positive influence on the car's value now. Heated rear screens for Saloons and Travellers, improved heating, strengthened half shafts, brake servos and the fitting of unleaded cylinder heads are all items to put a tick against. Anything that improves the comfort levels has got to be seen as a benefit, unless, of course, originality is even more of a priority. Inevitably, this will be a matter of personal preference.

Undesirable extras

The shortcomings of the semaphore indicators, and the interim flashing indicator system which used the brake lights have led a variety of alternative permanent and semi-permanent systems being adopted for safety reasons. If these have been fitted to the bodywork and, in the process, required additional holes to be drilled, then there may be cost implications if there is a desire to return to original specification, albeit with a temporary detachable system fitted.

Half thought-out performance enhancing modifications should be seriously reviewed. Examples such as installing an uprated 1275/1300cc engine without making corresponding changes to the braking system is ill-advised. It could compromise your chances of getting insurance cover.

Restoration photographs

Any supporting evidence to authenticate the claims of the vendor regarding restoration, service history or the acquisition of new parts should be carefully examined. Photographs in particular are a useful record and significantly add to the provenance of the vehicle. Enquire if the photos or copies will be part of the sale.

Striking a deal

Having carefully assessed the condition of the car and calculated the cost of any rectifying work you feel will be necessary, consider how this compares with your budget and the asking price. Most asking prices are set with a degree of negotiation expected, but don't be frightened to walk away if you are not sure.

13 Do you really want to restore?
— it will take longer and cost more than you think

Before: would you tackle this?   After: would you buy it now to finish?

One of the biggest dilemmas when buying a Morris Minor is whether to spend your hard earned cash or inheritance on buying the best condition car available at the time, or to take on a cheaper car needing considerable work, or even a full restoration. The decision may be influenced by a number of factors: the rarity of the vehicle, the challenge of completing a restoration to the standard you want, or the fact that it is a means of getting what you want by spreading the cost over a longer period of time.

One thing is for certain, if you decide to embark on a restoration, the biggest single expense will not be the initial cost of the vehicle, or the parts needed. It will almost certainly be the labour costs involved, particularly if you are intending to employ the services of a professional restorer.

Assuming you are not skilled in all facets of restoration, there are a number of factors to consider when deciding who will do the restoration. Firstly, do you know anything about the company or individual? Have you seen any examples of the work they have done on other similar cars? Do they have any genuine letters of recommendation from satisfied customers? Are they located close enough to you so that you can keep a regular check on progress?

Once you have agreed who to employ, it is imperative that you make it crystal clear what it is you want doing. Making assumptions that the restorer can read your mind is a recipe for disaster. Spell it out if you want a nuts and bolts rebuild with a bare metal respray, and all glass removed. Advise on the new old stock panels you want, including any you will supply yourself. Have an open and ongoing dialogue with the restorer, but bear in mind, they have work to do and will charge for their time.

Neglected engine – cheaper to put right than structural metalwork.

Perhaps the most important issue to address is cost. Get a detailed quotation and ensure that once you commission the work, the costs are binding. Agree at the outset that if unforeseen work is necessary, you will be consulted before the work is undertaken and any additional costs are incurred. Agreeing staged payments is a useful way of keeping things on track and allows for ongoing quality assurance checks. Finally, have a realistic target date for completion. Restorers are often too optimistic in their assessment of how long things will take, and this can create tension and cause frustration.

For some, a home restoration is a real possibility, even if you have to take time out to acquire or brush up on essential skills such as welding and painting. Such undertakings can be extremely rewarding but tend to be open-ended. Pressure on relationships is a consideration, as many hours will be required to complete all the work. Having good facilities and the proper tools and equipment, either bought, borrowed or hired, will influence the final quality of the work. Sustaining interest in long term projects or rolling restoration while the vehicle remains in use is difficult. This is the main contributory factor to so many part-finished restoration projects being offered for sale … often at considerable financial loss!

Replacement front chassis legs are available in half and full sized versions. It's an expensive undertaking which requires the front suspension to be dismantled.

On the positive side, there are hundreds, if not thousands, of well-restored Morris Minors which have been completed. There is a good supply of parts, a wealth of knowledge and experience to draw on, and a thriving community all determined to support endeavours to keep the Minor on the road.

Safety should always be the prime consideration when working beneath the car. A mounting jig that allows the car to be rolled on to its side, as shown, is a good investment in terms of safe access and making repair work much easier.

Paintwork problems can detract from the overall appearance of a vehicle and seriously undermine its value. There is a strong possibility that the vehicle you are looking at will have been repainted at least once and, in some cases, more often than this.

Orange peel

The presence of an orange peel effect in the paintwork, so-called because it resembles the skin of an orange, is indicative of the fact that remedial paintwork or a full respray has occurred at some point. The cause is mainly down to uneven application of paint. If it is not too serious, it can be cut back using proprietary paint cutting products or rubbing compounds. Failing that, the affected panels or the whole vehicle will need to be repainted.

A classic case of paint blistering due to rust. It is not always as obvious, or advanced as this.

Cracking

Too heavy an application of paint or too many coats can result in severe cracking. Cracks can also be symptomatic of other problems, including the presence of filler beneath the paint. Another cause can be the application of one type of paint on top of another without the use of an appropriate isolater.

Fading

Certain colours used on Morris Minors are prone to fading. Two in particular are worthy of checking; Maroon and Rose Taupe. Applying paint restoring compounds can bring back some lustre to the paint, but often the only real solution is a complete respray.

Paint blistering due to metal corrosion with evidence of the underlying problem.

Blistering

A common occurrence on older vehicles that is caused almost exclusively by the corrosion of the underlying metal. Inevitably, the damage will be more widespread than the blistering suggests. The only solution is to repair or replace the metal in the affected area, prior to repainting.

Microblistering

A result of the vehicle being subjected to an economy respray: inadequate heating allows moisture to build up on the surface of the vehicle before painting. It can also be caused by the protracted use of car covers that do not 'breathe'. Seek advice from a paint specialist. Usually a full or partial respray will be necessary.

15 Problems due to lack of use
– just like their owners, Morris Minors need exercise!

Lack of use can cause major problems for any classic car. In the case of the Morris Minor, there are a number of problems to look out for.

Hydraulic problems
Brake fluid is hydroscopic (it absorbs water). If a vehicle is left unused for a long time, this process can adversely affect braking performance. In extreme circumstances, it can cause brake failure. It is strongly recommended that brake fluid is changed every two years.

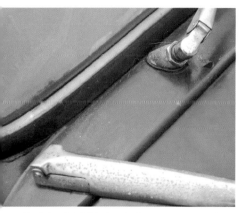

Perished rubbers may be a precursor to water ingress, wet carpets and rusting floors.

Beware of cracked sidewalls even if tyres do reinflate. Also, flat spots can result from long periods of standing.

Engine fluids
Even the well-respected A-Series engine is susceptible to problems through lack of use. Old engine oil becomes acidic which can have an adverse effect on engine bearings and other internal components.

Uninhibited coolant can also create major problems if left unattended for prolonged periods. Lack of antifreeze can cause core plugs to be pushed out and cylinder heads and engine blocks to crack. Silting up and solidification of deposited materials can cause overheating.

Rubber components
Rubber components perish and crack with age and lack of use. This can cause difficulties with steering and suspension parts, as well as window and door seals, and radiator/heater hoses.

Wheels and tyres
Vehicles which have stood for long periods of time usually have problems associated with the tyres, which inevitably have borne all the weight. Cracks in the tyre sidewalls and flat spots on the treads can contribute to associated problems such as steering vibration.

Electrics
- Batteries which are not used regularly will fail completely if left uncharged.
- Wiring insulation in older cars may harden and become brittle.
- Connectors like those used on the fuse box on all Morris Minors will corrode if left unused.

Lack of use may, in extreme cases, be signified by excessive plant growth!

Traveller wood
Neglected Traveller wood is a significant problem as the ingress of water into the joints causes the onset of rot. This is indicated by discolouration and some softening of the wood at key structural points. Some people mistakenly view the wood as decorative. Others are unaware of its vital role in holding the car together!

Rotting exhaust systems
Exhaust gases have a high water content. Consequently, exhaust systems corrode very quickly when a vehicle is not in use for a long time.

Extended storage
Cars placed in storage for extended periods of time can suffer problems as a result of components degenerating. A good example is the Bakelite steering wheel on early cars. If it's bad enough, it will disintegrate to a point where it's incapable of use until restored. Worse still, irreparable damage to seats and carpets can occur if storage conditions are poor.

Hoods (soft tops)
Deterioration of hood frames and covers can result from lack of use. This is particularly true of plastic hoods with celluloid rear windows, which can crack and split. Damage can also occur at the point where the hood is tensioned against the metal frame. Apart from fading badly, mohair canvas and PVC hoods do not take kindly to being stored in damp conditions. The fabric will rot quickly in these circumstances.

UK clubs

Morris Minor Owners Club
Liz Saxon, PO Box 1098, Derby, DE73
6WL.
Tel 01332 291675
www.mmoc.org.uk

Cornwall Morris Minor 1000 Club
Brian Herbert, 40 Penwethers Lane,
Truro, Cornwall, TR1 3PW.
www.cornwallmorrisminorclub.co.uk

LCV Register
Brian Lee.
45 Frederick Road, Warley, West
Midlands, B68 0NX.
www.minorlcvreg.co.uk

Europe

Denmark

Nordisk Morris Minor Klubb
Simon Marsboll, Gl. Kongevej 16, DK
– 7442 Engesvang, Denmark.
Tel: 45 8686 5774
www.nmmk.dk

France

Amicale Morris Minor France
Chris & Mary Hall, Rue Paul Tourseiller,
46700, Puy L'Eveaue, Duravel, France.
Tel: 33 565 24 66 46

Germany

Morris Minor Registry Deutschland
Eckard Blocher, President
35687 Dillenburg
Germany
www.morrisminor.de

Holland

Morris Minor Club Netherland
Henk Van Galen, Nilantsweg 37,
Anton Visser, Zwolle, 8041 AP, The
Netherlands.
Tel: 030 261 2359
www.morrisminorclub.nl

Italy

Italian Morris Minor Owners Club
Via R. Fucini 204, 00137 Rome, Italy.

Switzerland

Swiss Morris Minor Club
Herr. H-U Gubser, Feldbergstrasse 86,
4057 Basel, Switzerland.
Tel. 061 693 44 88
www.morrisminor.ch

Overseas

USA

Morris Minor Registry
Tony Burgess, 318 Hampton Park,
Westerville, OH 43081 – 5723, USA.
Tel. 014 899 2394
http://members.aol.com/morrisminr

Australia

MMCCV Inc
The Secretary, P O Box 354, Balwyn,
Victoria 3103, Australia.
www.vicnet.net.au

Morris Minor Car Club of NSW Inc
P O Box 605, Granville NSW 2142,
Australia.

Wollongong Morris Minor Car Club
41 Williamson Street, Corrimal NSW
2518, Australia.

**Morris Minor Owners Club of
Tasmania Inc**
PO Box 783, Devonport, Tasmania
7310.

New Zealand

Morris Minor Car Club New Zealand
Alan Hoverd, 68 Liardet Street,
Mornington, Wellington 6002, New
Zealand.

Auckland Morris Minor Car Club
PO Box 29, 216 Greenwoods Corner,
Auckland, 1003, New Zealand.
www.morrisminor.co.nz

South Africa

Morris Minor Owners Club of South Africa

13 Van Wouw Street, Groenkloof, Pretoria 0181, South Africa.

Specialists

Repairs

Bristol Classic Motorcars

Richmond Road Garage, Richmond Road, St George, Bristol.
Tel: 0117 9413612

Carsmiths

Old Station Yard, Chapel Street, Cawston, Norwich, NR10 4BG.
Tel: 01603 872568

Goddard Engineering

Rhyddnant, Sennybridge, Brecon, South Wales LD3 8TN.
Tel: 01874 624600
www.goddardengineering.com

Minor Magic

'Three Bridges', Bradford-on-Tone, Taunton, Devon TA4 1EN.
Tel: 01823 461861
www.minormagic.co.uk

Minor Services

Ian Allen, 53 Main Street, Witchford, Ely, Cambridgeshire CB6 2HG.
Tel: 01353 662485

Pop's Place

Richard Talbot, 121 High Road, Wortwell, Norfolk IP20 0EN.
Tel: 01379 741409
www.pops-place.co.uk

Roy's Welding

1 Forest Road, Feltham, Middlesex TW13 7RR.
Tel: 01747 830499

SGA Motors

4A Morant Road, Ringwood, Hampshire BH24 1SX.
Tel: 01425 461241

Spares/repairs

LMG Kent Ltd, 21 Upland Road, Bexleyheath, Kent, DA7 4NR.
Tel: 020 8303 4811 or 020 8303 2593
www.lmgkent.co.uk

London Repair Centre

Unit 5, Victoria Wharf Ind. Estate, Grove Street, Deptford, London SE8 3QQ.
Tel: 020 8692 9544
www.minoradjustments.co.uk

Minor Mania

1-3 Hale Lane, Mill Hill, London NW7 3NU.
Tel: 0800 074 5852
www.minor-mania.co.uk

Minor Medics

Units 27/28 Lodge Farm, Castlethorpe, Milton Keynes.
Tel: 01908 510736

Bull Motif Spares

Reardene Workshops, Cleeve Road, Middle Littleton, Worcestershire WR11 8JR.
Tel: 01386 831755
www.bullmotif.com

DSN Classics

Bunns Bank Ind. Est, Attleborough, Norfolk, NR17 1QD.
Tel: 01953 455551
www.dsnclassics.co.uk

Leadbetters of Lancashire

329/331 Preston Road, Clayton-Le-Woods, Nr. Chorley, Lancashire PR6 7PY.
Tel: 01257 275314

MGM Spares

151 Ormskirk Road, Newtown, Wigan.
Tel: 01942 820181
Fax: 01942 820920
Broomhouse Lane Ind. Estate, Doncaster.
Tel: 01709 864964
Fax: 01709 864278
www.mgm-spares.co.uk

Spares

Minor Developments
John Vine, 2 Mill Lane, Hoobrook,
Kidderminster, Worcestershire
DY10 1BR.
Tel: 01562 747718

Morris Minor Centre (B'ham) Ltd
993 Wolverhampton Road, Oldbury,
West Midlands, B69 4RJ.
Tel: 0121 544 5522
www.morrisminor.co.uk

Morris Minor Parts Centre (London)
143 Cannon Hill Lane, Raynes Park,
London, SW20 9BZ.
Tel: 020 8543 2264

Morris Surplus
213 Chaseside, Enfield, Middlesex
EN2 0RA.
Tel: 07768 734339

Gearboxes

Classic Gearbox (re-builds)
Peter Cavanagh, 1 Stanley Avenue,
Marple, Cheshire, SK6 6JJ.
Tel: 0161 427 4442 or 07788 572 315

John E Evans
24 Seaview Road, Hayling Island,
Hants PO11 9PE.
Tel: 02392 465256

Wordwork

S T Foreman (Woodies)
Unit 25, Eastmead Ind. Estate, Lavant,
Chichester, West Sussex, PO18 0DB.
Tel: 01243 788660
www.morriswoodwork.co.uk

Traveller Timbers
5 The Close, Little Weighton, Hull,
East Yorkshire HU20 3XA.
Tel: 01482 846787
www.travellertimbers.co.uk

Others

Canterbury Convertibles (Minor Convertibles)
Broomfield, Preston Hill, Wingham,
Nr. Canterbury CT3 1DB.
Tel: 01227 720306
www.morrisminorconvertible.co.uk

Cover Systems (car covers)
49 Grove Road, Rushden, NN10 0YD.
Tel: 01933 410851

P J Covers (car covers)
5 Holcombe Road, Teignmouth, South
Devon, TQ14 8UP.
Tel: 01626 775091
www.pj-covers.co.uk

Newton Commercial (interior trim)
Eastlands Industrial Estate, Leiston,
Suffolk, IP16 4LL.
Tel: 01728 832880
www.newtoncomm.co.uk

AON Limited (insurance)
Tel: 08705 70 80 90

RAC (breakdown/windscreen repairs)
Tel: 0800 716 976

Books

Morris Minor and 1000 Superprofile
– Ray Newell, Haynes/Foulis, 1982
Morris Minor Series MM Superprofile
– Ray Newell, Haynes/Foulis, 1984
Morris Minor The Shire Album – Ray
Newell, 1992, 1995, 1998, 2000.
Original Morris Minor Bay View Books
– Ray Newell, 1992, revised 1995.
Morris Minor The First Fifty Years – Ray
Newell, Bay View Books, 1997.
Morris Minor The Complete Story,
Crowood Press, 1998.
The World's Supeme Small Car – Paul
Skilleter, Osprey, 3rd Edition 1989.
Morris Minor Restoration – Jim Tyler,
Osprey, 1995.
Exploring The Legend – Jon Pressnell,
Haynes, 1998
Secret Life of the Morris Minor – Karen
Pender, Veloce Publishing

17 Vital statistics
– essential data at your fingertips

Morris Minor Series II	Built: Cowley, England, 1952-1956
Total number built: 269,838	

Engine: Cast iron block and cylinder head. Pressed steel sump. Four cylinders set in-line with overhead valves.	**Capacity:** 803cc
	Bore & stroke: 58mm x 76mm
	Compression: 7.2:1
Carburettor: Single S.U. H1 type, 1⅛in	**Maximum torque:** 40lb/ft at 2400rpm
Fuel pump: S.U. type L	**Maximum power:** 30bhp at 4800rpm
Air cleaner: Dry gauze type	

Transmission: Rear wheel drive from front mounted engine. 4-speed gearbox bolted to rear engine plate. Synchromesh on 2nd, 3rd and top gears. Clutch, Borg and Beck 6¼in dry plate	**Gear ratios:** Reverse 5.174:1, First 4.09:1, Second 2.588:1, Third 1.679:1, Top 1.000:1
	Overall ratios: Reverse 27.38:1, First 21.618:1, Second 13.69:1, Third 8.88:1, Top 5.286:1
Final drive: Hypoid axle 7/37. Two pinion differential. Final drive ratio 5.286:1	

Dimensions & weight:	Overall width:	Overall length:	Overall height:
2-door Saloon (15 cwt)	5ft 1in	12ft 4in	5ft 0in
4-door Saloon (15¾ cwt)Convertible (15 cwt)	5ft 1in	12ft 4in	5ft 0in
	5ft 1in	12ft 4in	5ft 0in
Traveller (16½ cwt)	5ft 1in	12ft 5in	5ft 0in
Ground clearance: 6¾in			

Wheelbase & track: Wheelbase 7ft 2in. Track – Front 4ft 2⅝in, Rear 4ft 2⁵⁄₁₆in	
Suspension: Front – Independent by torsion bars and links. Rear – Half-elliptic leaf springs	**Steering:** Rack and pinion. 2½ turns lock-to-lock. Turning circle, 33ft
Brakes: Lockheed hydraulic, 7in diameter drums. Front, two leading shoes. Rear, one leading and one trailing shoe	**Wheels & tyres:** 14in pressed steel disc. 4-bolt fixings. Tyres, 5.00x14
Bodywork: Designed by Issigonis, unitary all steel construction, assembled at Cowley. 2-door and 4-door Saloons, Convertible and Traveller available. Traveller rear section constructed with external ash frame and aluminium panelling, including roof	**Electrical system:** Positive earth, 12V, 43amp/hr. battery mounted on tray in engine bay. Positive earth. Lucas dynamo type C39PV/2 with Lucas compensated voltage control box and coil ignition. Headlamps Lucas double dip 42/36W. Semaphore trafficators 3W
Performance: Maximum speed 62mph. Maximum speed in gears: 1st 18mph, 2nd 30mph, 3rd 45mph	**Acceleration:** 0-30 8.5 secs, 0-40 15.1 secs, 0-50 29.2 secs, 0-60 52.5 secs; standing ¼-mile 27.1 secs
Fuel consumption: 36-40mpg	

Car identification

The car (chassis) number appears on the identification plate which is mounted on the right-hand side of the dash panel next to the main wiring harness grommet aperture. The practice of recording engine numbers changed throughout production. On very early models, the engine number was stamped on a disc attached to the flywheel housing. It also appeared on the identification plate. On other models the engine number was stamped on a plate secured to the right-hand side of the cylinder block above the dynamo mounting bracket. It also appeared on the identification plate. On 1098cc models, it only appeared on the cylinder block.

From April 1952 until September 1962, car (chassis) numbers were prefixed by an identification code consisting of three letters and two numbers. The first letter indicates the make and model (F = Morris Minor); the second letter indicates the body type (eg A = 4-door Saloon, B = 2-door Saloon); the third letter indicates the colour in which the vehicle is finished (eg A = Black); the first number indicates the class to which the vehicle belongs (eg 1 = RHD Home Market, 2 = RHD Export); the second number indicates the type of paint used to finish the vehicle (eg 1 = Synthetic, 2 = Synobel, 3 = Cellulose). Thus: FBA13 = Morris Minor, 2-door Saloon, black, produced as right-hand drive for the home market and finished in cellulose paint. Note: The second number denoting paint type was not always used on later models.

From September 1962 until production ended a different car number identification code prefix was used. This consisted of three letters and one figure, followed by an additional letter if the vehicle differed from standard right-hand drive.

The first letter denotes the make of the vehicle (M = Morris); the second letter denotes the model's engine type (A = A-Series engine); the third letter denotes the body type (S – 4 door Saloon, 2S – 2 door Saloon, W – dual purpose, T – 4 seater tourer); the fourth prefix (a number) denotes the series of model – indicating a major change (post-1962 vehicles fifth series); the fifth prefix denotes vehicles which differ from standard RHD (L = Left-hand drive, D = Deluxe). Thus: MA2S5 = Morris 1000, right-hand drive, standard 2-door Saloon, fifth series. Note: Dates and car number change points are, in some cases, approximate as the manufacturers sometimes incorporated modifications before, or after, the 'official' change point. Where major production changes occurred, change points have been included for all models. Elsewhere the earliest known change point is given.

Production modifications

While production changes are detailed for ohv engine models only, it is worth noting that the first Morris Minor in production was a 2-door Saloon car number SMM 501. It was October 1950 when the first 4-door Saloon became available and headlights were fitted in the wings for the first time (car number SMM 62551).

August 1952: First ohv engine fitted in 4-door Saloon (sidevalve engines continued in some), 160001.
January 1953: All models fitted with ohv engine, 180001.
October 1953: New model designated 'Traveller' introduced, 216901. Deluxe models featured a heater, leather seats, over-riders and passenger sun visor. 2-door Saloon, 221842. 4-door Saloon, 221803. Convertible, 221914.
January 1954: 'A' type rear axle and standard swivel pin assembly introduced, 228267. Wedge-type fan belt at engine no. 72610.
June 1954: Engine steady cable, 264013.
October 1954: Horizontal grille bars introduced. Revised instrument and control

Morris Minor 1000, 948cc	**Built:** Cowley, England, 1956-1962. Travellers assembled at Abingdon 1960-1962.
Total number built: 554,048	

Engine: Cast iron block and cylinder head. Pressed steel sump. 4 cylinders in line, overhead valves pushrod operated	**Capacity:** 948cc
	Bore & stroke: 62.9mm x 76.2mm
	Compression: 78.3:1 (High compression engine)
Carburettor: S.U. H2 type, 1¼in	**Maximum torque:** 50lb/ft at 2500rpm
Fuel pump: S.U. type L	**Maximum power:** 37bhp at 4750rpm
Air cleaner: A.C. t	

Transmission: Rear wheel drive from front mounted engine. 4-speed gearbox bolted to rear engine plate. Remote control gearchange. Synchromesh on 2nd, 3rd and top gears. Clutch, Borg and Beck 6¼in dry plate	**Gear ratios:** Reverse 4.664:1, First 3.628:1, Second 2.374:1, Third 1.412:1, Top 1.000:1
	Overall ratios: Reverse21.221:1, First 16,507:1, Second 10.802:1, Third 6.425:1, Top 4.555:1
Final drive: three quarter floating rear axle. Hypoid final drive 9/41, ratio 4.55:1	

Dimensions & weight:	Overall width:	Overall length:	Overall height:
2-door Saloon (15½ cwt)	5ft 1in	12ft 4in	5ft 0in
4-door Saloon (15¾ cwt)	5ft 1in	12ft 4in	5ft 0in
Convertible (15 cwt)	5ft 1in	12ft 4in	5ft 0in
Traveller (16½ cwt)	5ft 1in	12ft 5in	5ft 0in
Ground clearance: 6¾in			

Wheelbase & track: Wheelbase 7ft 2in. Track – Front 4ft 2⅝in, Rear 4ft 2⁵⁄₁₆in	
Suspension: Front – Independent by torsion bars and links. Rear – Half-elliptic leaf springs	**Steering:** Rack and pinion. 2½ turns lock-to-lock. Turning circle, 33ft
Brakes: Lockheed hydraulic, 7in diameter drums. Front, two leading shoes. Rear, one leading and one trailing shoe	**Wheels & tyres:** 14in pressed steel disc. 4-stud fixing. Tyres, 5.00x14 tubeless
Bodywork: Designed by Issigonis, all steel unitary construction. 2/4-door Saloons and Convertibles assembled at Cowley. Travellers assembled at Abingdon from 1960. Traveller constructed with external ash frame for rear section and aluminium panelling, including roof	**Electrical system:** Positive earth, 12V, 43amp battery mounted on tray in engine bay. Positive earth Lucas dynamo type C39PV/2 with Lucas compensated voltage control box and coil ignition. Headlamps Lucas double dip 42/36W. Semaphore trafficators 3W
Performance: Maximum speed 75.1mph. Maximum speed in gears: 1st 23.4mph, 2nd 35.2mph, 3rd 60.5mph	**Acceleration:** 0-30 6.8 secs, 0-40 12.1 secs, 0-50 18.5 secs, 0-60 30.0 secs; standing ¼-mile 24.2 secs
Fuel consumption: 37-44mpg	

panel. Separate speedometer, fuel and oil pressure gauges replaced by single separate instrument with open gloveboxes each side, 286441. 2-door Saloon, 291140. 4-door Saloon, 290173. Convertible, 291336. Traveller, 289687. New larger rear light fitting incorporating reflector in lens cover fitted, 293051.

August 1956: Coloured hoods fitted to Convertible, 422571.

October 1956: Series II discontinued. Final chassis number 448714.

October 1956: Standard and Deluxe 2- and 4-door Saloons. Convertible and Traveller introduced, designated "Minor 1000". 948cc engine fitted. Single piece curved windscreen and larger rear window. Dished steering wheel. Horn and trafficator control on steering column. Glovebox lids fitted. Deeper rear wings. Shorter gearlever. "Minor 1000" motif on sides of bonnet, 448801.

December 1956: New strengthened steering swivel pin assembly fitted, 462458.

March 1957: Fuel tank enlarged from 5 to 6 gallons, 487048 Saloon, Traveller, 485127.

September 1957: Canvas hood on Convertible replaced by plastic coated material, 524944.

November 1957: Gearlever reset and lengthened. Traveller, 552906. Other models, 557451.

October 1958: Courtesy light switches fitted in front doors, 654750.

December 1958: Rear spring design changed from 7 x ¼in leaves to 5 x ¼in leaves, 680464.

February 1959: Early type dry paper element air cleaner, car 698137. Traveller, 693918.

March 1959: Wider opening doors, self-cancelling direction indicator switch fitted to steering column. Horn button moved to centre of steering wheel. Traveller, 704254. 4-door Saloon, 705224. 2 door Saloon, 705622.

September 1959: Combined inlet and exhaust manifold. Foot space between gearbox cover and clutch pedal increased. PVC interior roof lining fitted instead of cloth. Front passenger seat on 2-door Saloon and Traveller modified to give better access to rear seats, 750470.

During 1960: HS type SU carburettor introduced. Engine number 9 M/U/H. 353449.

January 1961: Morris Minor 1,000,000 produced as special edition of 349 cars. Special features included lilac colour, white upholstery with black piping, "Minor 1,000,000" badging on sides of bonnet and on boot lid, plus special wheel rim embellishers. 1,000,000-1,000,349, (these car numbers designated out of sequence).

October 1961: Flashing direction indicators incorporated in front and rear lamps. Semaphore type direction indicators discontinued. Glove compartment lid removed. Windscreen washers fitted on Deluxe models. Seatbelt anchorage points built in to all models. New range of colours and upholstery offered. 2-door Saloon, 925555. 4-door Saloon, 925448. Convertible, 947088. Traveller, 925679.

September 1962: 948cc engine. Series discontinued. Final chassis numbers: 2-door Saloon, 990288. 4-door Saloon, 990283. Convertible, 989679. Traveller, 990289.

April 1963: Fresh air heater introduced. Air intake on radiator cowl. Redesigned windscreen washer system, 1039564.

October 1963: Windscreen wiper blades lengthened and now work in tandem. Zone toughened windscreen introduced. New design combined side/flasher lamps at front and rear. Extra round amber light fitted to rear of Traveller. New type air cleaner fitted to prevent carburettor icing in cold weather. N/S door lock fitted to 2-door models. 2-door Saloon, 1043218. 4-door Saloon, 1043752. Convertible, 1043271. Traveller, 1043226.

October 1964: New design facia panel. Better trim and more comfortable seating.

Morris Minor 1000, 1098cc	Built: Cowley, England, 1962-1971. Travellers assembled at Abingdon 1960-1962
Total number built: 303,443	

Engine: Cast iron block and cylinder head. Pressed steel sump. 4 cylinders in line, overhead valves pushrod operated	**Capacity:** 1098cc
	Bore & Stroke: 64.58mm x 83.72mm
	Compression: 8.5:1 (High compression engine)
Carburettor: S.U. HS2 type, 1¼in	**Maximum Torque:** 60lb/ft at 2500rpm
Fuel Pump: S.U. type L	**Maximum Power:** 48bhp at 5100rpm
Air Cleaner: Cooper dry type, with paper element	**Oil Filter:** Full-flow, with paper element

Transmission: Rear wheel drive from front mounted engine. 4-speed gearbox bolted to rear engine plate. Remote control gearchange. Synchromesh on 2nd, 3rd and top gears. Clutch, 7¼in dry plate	**Gear ratios:** Reverse 4.664:1, First 3.628:1, Second 2.172:1, Third 1.412:1, Top 1.000:1
	Overall ratios: Reverse 19.665:1, First 15.276:1, Second 9.169:1, Third 5.950:1, Top 4.220:1
Final Drive: three quarter floating rear axle. Hypoid final drive 9/38, ratio 4.22:1	

Dimensions & Weight:	Overall width:	Overall length:	Overall height:
2-door Saloon (15½ cwt)	5ft 1in	12ft 4in	5ft 0in
4-door Saloon (15¾ cwt)	5ft 1in	12ft 4in	5ft 0in
Convertible (15 cwt)	5ft 1in	12ft 4in	5ft 0in
Traveller (16½ cwt)	5ft 1in	12ft 5in	5ft 0in
Ground clearance: 6¾in			

Wheelbase & Track: Wheelbase 7ft 2in. Track – Front 4ft 2⅝in, Rear 4ft 2⁵⁄₁₆in

Suspension: Front – Independent by torsion bars and links. Rear – Half-elliptic leaf springs	**Steering:** Rack and pinion. 2½ turns lock-to-lock. Turning circle, 33ft
Brakes: Lockheed hydraulic. Front 8in diameter drums. Rear 7in diameter drums. Front, two leading shoes. Rear, one leading shoe, one trailing shoe	**Wheels & Tyres:** 14in pressed steel disc. 4-stud fixing. Tyres, 5.20x14 tubeless
Bodywork: Designed by Issigonis, all steel unitary construction. 2/4 door Saloons and Convertibles assembled at Cowley. 1962-64 Travellers assembled at Abingdon	**Electrical System:** Positive earth, 12V, 43amp/hr. battery mounted on tray in engine bay. Positive earth Lucas dynamo type C40-1 with Lucas control box RB106/2 and coil. Ignition Lucas LA12. Flashing indicator unit Lucas FL5. Headlamps Lucas double dip 42/36W
Performance: Maximum speed 78mph. Maximum speed in gears: 1st 27.5mph, 2nd 41.5mph, 3rd 68mph	**Acceleration:** 0-30 6.4 secs, 0-40 9.8 secs, 0-50 15.8 secs, 0-60 24.2 secs; standing ¼-mile 22.9 secs
Fuel consumption: 40-45mpg	

Automatic boot lid support. Glovebox on passenger side fitted with lid. Combined ignition and starter switch. Other switches modified. Swivel ashtrays under parcel shelf. Crushable sun visors. Plastic rimmed interior mirror. Two spoke safety dished steering wheel. Fresh air heater performance improved. 2-door Saloon, 1082280. 4-door Saloon, 1082284. Convertible, 1082717. Traveller, 1082537.

October 1966: Sealed beam headlamps fitted. Fuse in sidelamp circuit introduced, 1159663.

October 1967: New type of paper air cleaner element introduced, 1196653.

June 1969: Convertible discontinued. Final car number 1254328.
Late 1969: Oil filter switch ceased to be fitted. Amber warning lens fitted but not used.
1970: During the last months of production, some models were fitted with an alternator instead of a dynamo.
November 1970: Saloon production discontinued. Final car numbers, 2-door Saloon, 1288377. 4-door Saloon, 1288299.
1971: During the last months of production, some of the vehicles assembled at the Morris Commercial Cars plant at Adderley Park, Birmingham, were fitted with steering column ignition locks.
April 1971: Traveller production discontinued. Final car number 1294082.

Post-production Convertibles
Essential checks
Determining whether a Convertible is a genuine vehicle or converted Saloon is relatively straightforward unless someone has gone to a lot of trouble to conceal the change. Here is a quick checklist.

Registration
Convertible production stopped in 1969. Post-1969 registrations are an early warning sign.

Documentation
If you have the original chassis number and prefix this can be checked with original factory records.

Some unscrupulous people have changed registration documents and made up new chassis plates.

Vehicle checks
The strengthening pieces at each end of the dash panel and at the B post on top of the inner sill were originally spot welded in place. Almost all converted Saloons have these seams welded in.

With the kick plates removed, it should be possible to see that an extra strengthening piece has recently been welded in.

Some evidence of where the roof has been cut off should remain visible in the area behind the rear seat.

There will be a slight variation in the header rail above the windscreen, compared with an original Convertible.

It should be noted that, converted correctly, a Saloon can be just as safe and equally attractive as a genuine Convertible.

M O'DOWD & SONS

Retro

Auto

**Unit 26 Heath Hill Industrial Estate
Dawley, Telford, Shropshire, TF2 0DZ**

Repairs   **Servicing**

Restoration

01952 505900

www.retroauto.co.uk

*Martin & Robert are pleased to have been
of assistance to the author of this book.*

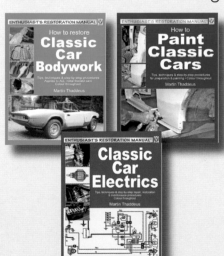

The **Essential** Buyer's Guide™ Series

Alfa Romeo Giulia GT Coupé
ISBN: 978-1-904788-69-0

Alfa Romeo Giulia Spider
ISBN: 978-1-904788-98-0

Citroën 2CV
ISBN: 978-1-845840-99-0

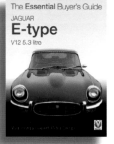

Jaguar/ Daimler XJ6, XJ12 & Sovereign
ISBN: 978-1-845841-19-5

Jaguar E-type 3.8 & 4.2 litre
ISBN: 978-1-904788-85-0

Jaguar E-type V12 5.3 litre
ISBN: 978-1-845840-77-8

MGB & MGB GT
ISBN: 978-1-845840-29-7

Mercedes-Benz 280-560SL & SLC – W107 series Roadsters & Coupés 1971 to 1989
ISBN: 978-1-845841-07-2

Porsche 928
ISBN: 978-1-904788-70-6

Triumph TR6
ISBN: 978-1-845840-26-6

Volkswagen Beetle
ISBN: 978-1-904788-72-0

Volkswagen Bus
ISBN: 978-1-845840-22-8

£9.99*/$19.99*

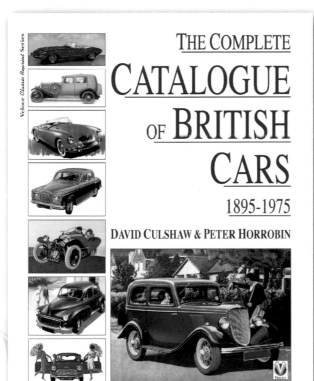

The most comprehensive account of British cars ever published in one volume, this book presents a huge amount of information – historical as well as technical – in a way which will serve the needs of the dedicated enthusiast, automotive historian and the general reader.

The Complete Catalogue of British Cars 1895-1975
by David Culshaw & Peter Horrobin

ISBN: 978-1-874105-93-0
£30.00*/$54.95*

Hardback • 496 pages • More than 1000 photographs

*prices subject to change. p&p extra. for more details visit www.veloce.co.uk or email info@veloce.co.uk.

Index